VISITING INDIA

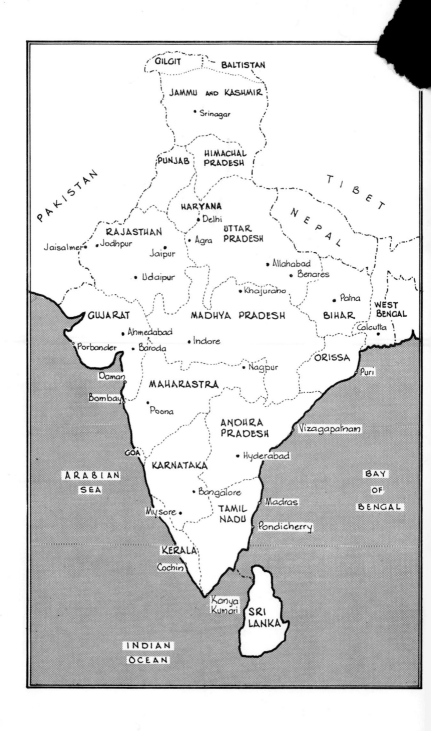

VISITING INDIA

Allan Stacey

B. T. Batsford Ltd London

To Peter Holloway

© Allan Stacey 1986

First published 1986

All rights reserved. No part of this publication
may be reproduced, in any form or by any means,
without permission from the Publisher

ISBN 0 7134 4724 9

Typeset by Latimer Trend & Company Ltd, Plymouth
and printed in Great Britain by
Butler & Tanner Ltd
Frome, Somerset
for the publishers
B. T. Batsford Ltd.
4 Fitzhardinge Street
London W1H 0AH

Contents

Introduction   9

I Background   13

India—the country · India—the beginnings ·
Population · Languages · States, capitals and
languages · States and their peoples ·
Government, the States and politics · Village India

II Religion   33

Hinduism · Islam · Buddhism · Jainism ·
Sikhism · Parsees

III Travel   45

General information · Travel in India · The railway
system · Air travel · Travel by road · Hill stations ·
Festivals and fairs · Some game sanctuaries ·
Healthy travel · Sensible eating and drinking ·
Photography

IV Flora and Fauna   76

Trees · Shrubs · Climbing plants · Birds

V Entertainment   86

Classical Indian music · Indian classical dancing ·
The cinema, television and video

VI Gazetteer   93

Jammu and Kashmir   ·   Punjab   ·   Haryana   ·
Himachal Pradesh   ·   Uttar Pradesh   ·   West Bengal   ·
Bihar   ·   Orissa   ·   North-Eastern Indian Territories and
Sikkim   ·   Rajasthan   ·   Gujarat   ·   Maharastra   ·
Madhya Pradesh   ·   Mandu   ·   Goa   ·   Karnataka   ·
Vijayanagar   ·   Andha Pradesh   ·   Kerala   ·   Tamil
Nadu   ·   Pondicherry

Glossary   184
Bibliography   189
Index   190

Acknowledgments

The author wishes to thank the Government of India Tourist Bureau for use of photographs (except nos. 6, 10, 22, 50, 53, 57, 59 and 63 which were taken by the author); also Peter Holloway for his invaluable advice and help in preparing the typescript and for the use of some of his photographs. The maps were provided by Robert Brien. The colour photographs were taken by the author.

Introduction

India is a nation of absolute contrasts; there seem to be no half measures. There is the merciless sun whose summer heat will split rock and make the flesh of men become like old parchment. The monsoon rains churn the land to mud, swell and flood the rivers and pour through palace and hovel regardless. City drains uproot so that filth and rats float round people's legs. In contrast, in the Indian wintertime, palaces and temples shimmer beneath the rain-washed skies; relief and hope are felt by city-street and farmland dwellers alike, and chaotic communication systems return almost to normal.

India basks in this winter radiance, confident that visitors will see their picture-book images come to life. The observant eye, though, will see shops full of radios and televisions and refrigerators, of silks and satins and jewels, marble, gold and all manner of foodstuffs alongside which stand lopsided cigarette stalls, pavement traders, fortune tellers with parrots in cages waiting to be freed to choose a card for the 'lucky' customer.

A double-decker bus will be halted by a street cow, and a sleek, air-conditioned car will hoot to overtake a camel train. At the railway station an engine will be sweating diesel fumes whilst, by its side, a stoked-up steam engine will fascinate some by its retrospectivity.

Arid hills of ancient stone; fertile fields of emerald rice; snow-clad Himalayan heights above hot tea gardens; deserts and jungles, perched villages of tribal people and dense cities tuned to cosmopolitan living; prince, pauper, priest and politician; all these and more go to compounding the charm and the mystery of India.

There are also more familiar aspects for the Westerner, such as the Kennel Club, the Flower Show, national football, the Yacht Club, disco-dancing, neon lights and skyscraper blocks and a vast middle-class consumer society which, regardless of caste or class, increasingly demands more of everything, from chocolate bars to motor cars.

It is almost impossible for an outsider to understand the mores of a country so vast and variable as India. Its internal differences equal the ethnic, cultural and social differences of the whole of Europe. Not surprisingly, there are people all over the world whose curiosity about the

1 Transplanting rice seedlings into water-filled paddy field

legend that is India is so compelling that only by going and seeing will reality replace conjecture.

Global communications have quickened and the world's economic patterns have changed so that riches have become widespread and underwrite the power and influence of a political proletariat.

The Independence of India was a momentous event that was not just the freeing of a country from British power: it was the gaining of freedom of action for many different groups of people within India of diverse religions, languages and cultures. In their new unity they had to accustom themselves not only to the changed circumstances of state and country, but eventually to internationality. India had to suffer a curious and increasingly affluent outside world insistent on writing about – and recording and photographing – its marvels and its miseries. It is debatable whether or not, at that time, India was ready to receive such a welter of attention. Now, though, India is very much a part of the twentieth-century world, playing a political and spiritual rôle within the possibilities open to her.

She has prepared, as no other country in her position has, facilities to receive and satisfy the most fastidious of travellers whilst at the same time keeping alive the less Westernized resorts and hotels.

The intention of this book is to explain some of the idiosyncrasies of the culture and the life of India which may perplex visitors. It is also hoped that, through the gazetteer section, visitors will be able to plan either personal tours in India or deviations from arranged tours to visit places that are in the vicinity that might otherwise be missed.

1 Background

India – the country

India extends from north of Kashmir in the Himalayas, 3218 km (2000 miles) southwards to Kanya Kumari (once called Cape Cormorin) where the waters of the Bay of Bengal, the Indian Ocean and the Arabian Sea meet; it is the Land's End of India. From west to east – that is, from the small, unimportant township of Kori Kreek on the Rann of Kutch near the border with Pakistan to the frontier town of Kahan near Burma – the distance is almost the same, 3218 km (2000 miles).

The enormous width of India is often forgotten, being overshadowed by the more popular statistic of its length. As one uses the expression 'from John O'Groats to Land's End' in Britain, so Indians express the same distance as 'from Kashmir to Kanya Kumari'. It is an easily understandable way of meaning any great distance. Pilgrims will tell of their travels 'from Kashmir to Kanya Kumari' and politicians will speak of benefits affecting the whole of India in the same terms.

The distance of the width of India has no such usage yet it encompasses areas that are legendary in both ancient and modern Indian history. These are the areas of the western State of Gujarat, the Gangetic Plain and, further east, Bengal; and it is from these regions, most particularly from Gujarat and Bengal, that most of the Indians come who travel and settle abroad.

As a comparison, India is nearly twenty times as large as Great Britain, is three-fifths the size of the USA and is as large as Europe without Russia.

Western people tend to think of India as a tropical country. The travel posters and, seemingly, all the travel literature support this belief, showing, as they do, hot and dusty city scenes, palm-fringed beaches and half-clad people near temples either by the sea or by the river; yet all of India is north of the equator. The Tropic of Cancer runs through the middle of the country, thus putting the upper half into the Temperate Zone; this includes the Gangetic Plain, parts of which are, for a third of the year, as cold as London or New York in November.

A convenient division of India can be made by separating it horizontally from north to south into roughly three parts. The first part would be the great Himalayan mountains, the second the lowlands through which run rivers such as the Indus, the Ganges and the Bramaputra, and the third, the plateau stretching from mid-India to the mountains of the south and, eventually, land's end.

The Himalayas curve across the north of India making an almost impenetrable rampart, and included amongst the ranges are such giants as Mount Everest and Kanchenjunga. There are few usable passes over the mountains, though there is a route which leads from Darjeeling to China and another from Leh (now a region more accessible as there has been much tourist development in this area over the last ten years) into south China. In the north-west, on the Afghan frontier, the passes are lower and are easier, and it is from this direction that India has been most often invaded. It is here that the well-known Khyber Pass is found, though this is now in Pakistan.

The plains of northern India stretch in a great curve from the Arabian Sea to the Bay of Bengal. This land consists of fertile soil washed down by the streams and rivers for thousands of years. This huge area is almost all flat; it is more than 3218 km (2000 miles) from end to end and has an average width of 322 km (200 miles). Two-thirds of India's population lives, or exists, on this vast plain.

Almost the whole of India south of the great plains is plateau country, with lines of mountains crossing it: the Vindhya, the Satpura and the Ajanta ranges. The plateau is highest in the south and west, sloping on the whole towards the east. The Western and Eastern Ghats fall to a glorious coastline that runs from Bombay around the southern tip and up again towards Calcutta, and most of these thousands of sandy miles is completely unspoilt and quite undeveloped.

Off the shores of India are the islands which are part of the Indian Union, the main groups being the Laccadive Islands in the Arabian Sea and the Andaman and the Nicobar Islands in the Bay of Bengal.

India – the beginnings

Before Independence and Partition, the westernmost great river was the Indus. It was here from the mouth of the river northwards that began the great civilization generally referred to as the Indus Civilization and more particularly as the Harappan Civilization.

The ruined cities of Harappa and Mohenjo-Daro are now within Pakistan, but there are sites of this early settling within India, one such being in Lotal in the State of Gujarat. Here one can see signs of urban living similar to those extant at Pompeii. There are drains and baths, street order, public buildings, trading posts and harbourages; for Lotal, now inland, was once a port whose inhabitants traded with the more northerly Harappans at Harappa and Mohenjo-Daro.

The people at Lotal sold or bartered the prized ornamental conch shells from the beaches of the Kathiawar Peninsula in return for chert or chalcedony which had travelled to Mohenjo-Daro from Afghanistan, or for lapis lazuli from Persia. Trading was also carried on with the Egyptians, who used chalcedony together with lapis, jasper and the more precious minerals, such as ruby, for carving scarabs and seals.

At Lotal industry and shipping was well established and economically organized so that society there flourished. Eventually, though, the continual natural disasters such as cyclone and flood, together with the ever-present need to protect themselves as a community, undermined the Harappans of Lotal to an extent where they ceased to exist as a single force in South Gujarat. They are afterwards thought to have blended into the developing northern India.

Over a long period (from 2000 BC) the Aryans invaded India until, by 1500 BC, the Harappan way of life is thought to have declined – but it had flourished for the better part of 2000 years. It might be thought that the Harappans would have protected their territory more fervently but it must be remembered that they had been doing this for centuries and had not adapted to new dangers that threatened them – a state of affairs that often spells doom for a people.

Originally from Caucasia, the Aryans were of fair skin, a distinct advantage in a dark-skinned country, and, moreover, they spoke widespread languages, giving them an economic superiority by being able to trade back along the routes they had taken to India. They bred cattle well and rode and managed horses, talents which gave them power in trade and in battle, and they brought with them their culture and traditions which, whether by force or attraction, were absorbed into India's own ancient tribal cultures. The result was a blending of races and of colour, a process which continues to this day.

The word 'Aryan' is an adjective applied to a fair-skinned people; it is not a racial term. It is used to describe the fair, warring tribes which invaded India. 'Aryan' has the meaning of 'kinsman'; one is reminded of the word 'Iran', which has the same derivative.

The Aryans moved eastward along the route of the River Ganges until they had control of the whole of northern India, where they subjected the dark-skinned Dravidians, as the local tribal people were called, to work as slaves. There is a theory that the Aryans invented the caste system in order, on the one hand, to preserve their racial identity, and on the other, to prevent inter-marriage with the dark-skinned inhabitants; but this is only a theory.

The people became known as Hindus – from the word 'Indus'. As they moved eastwards they prospered by exploiting such trophy as iron ore and other mineral deposits. They created industrial, educational and recreational centres across northern India from Indraprastha (now Delhi) to Pataliputra (now known as Patna, in the State of Bihar).

With this eastward surge, the west became neglected and the inevitable happened – invasion. First, from Persia, came Darius (521 BC) followed

2 Dravidians of South India carting coconut palm leaves used for roofing

by the Greek, Alexander of Macedon, in 326 BC at Taxila, a city now in Northern Pakistan, 32 km (20 miles) north of Rawalpindi.

For Alexander it was to be only a brief time in India. Exhausted by untold climatic and territorial tribulations, and notwithstanding his prowess as a leader, he returned to Persia, aged 33; only three years later he died at Babylon, near modern Baghdad.

Indian art and philosophy were influenced by Hellenism for a considerable time after Alexander; this influence was later passed on to European art and thinking through its increasing knowledge of Indian cultures.

In the south, the Dravidians were a dark-skinned people who pre-dated the Aryans. They had their own class system and religious rites, including spirit worship. These dark people of the south, whether in or out of serfdom, obeyed orders: they fought, paid their taxes, farmed and generally worked to the glory of their king. The Chola Kings of Tanjore left an incredible architectural legacy, especially in such temples as the Brihadesawara at Tanjore itself, as did the Pallava Kings of Kanchipuram; they built to last, as the vast gopurams, or gateways, to the temples of the south testify.

Population

One cannot escape from people when visiting India. Even in unlikely places such as high in the mountains or in the middle of the desert one will find communities somehow scraping a living. Religions and economics and the climate have much to do with the increasing population burden on India's resources.

The heat and the dust, the monsoon and the mud, chill nights and windy days and frosts that freeze the ink in a ball-point pen, and a searing heat that numbs the mind – all these are elements that have tempered the peoples all across India. The climate has starved them, baked them as though in an oven and has killed them, yet has wrought in them an irrepressible urge to survive – a survival that depends utterly on the family and its continuity.

Throughout this vast land people proliferate so speedily that no census could be accurate, a view expressed by a fellow traveller on a train. When I was discussing the population problem he said, 'One cannot know the exact number of our people, but give or take ten lakhs I would guess . . .'. As ten lakhs is one million, it is quite a lot to be inexact about, yet it is only one seven-hundredth part of the total population of India.

The population dominates the land, the politics and the daily life throughout India. Plainly there are too many people. Food distribution is now more efficient, medicine is available to most, and an increase in literacy has shown more people how to exist at differing levels than were thought of 20 years ago. Migration to the Gulf States is one such variation. Also the death rate has decreased and people certainly live longer; facts that make a programme of birth control a daunting undertaking, aside from any religious or family considerations which often dictate a family's growth.

A statistic in a weekly magazine relating to a projected change in State voting arrangements illuminated this population problem. The State was Karnataka, one of the four southern States, and the article stated that 98 babies are born in Karnataka every minute. This means over four million babies a month and 50 million a year. There are 16 main States in India, some large and some small, and if one multiplies this birth-rate, and there is no reason to believe that the rate is any less elsewhere in India, then one has the staggering fact that 800 million souls are born annually throughout only these 16 States! Infant mortality is great in India and, whilst it brings personal grief, it is a controlling element which, together with natural disasters such as flood, famines, cyclones and bitter cold, cuts the survival rate of all ages.

The latest census population statistics were those announced in 1981/2 when there was a total of 687 million Indian people. By now this total will be well over the 700 million mark and, remembering the same article in the weekly magazine, the author maintained that India's population by AD 2000 would have reached 1000 million.

Indians are not alone in loving statistics, yet however wide of the mark both the birth-rate of Karnataka and the population of India in AD 2000 are, there is truth in the assumptions, if recent history is anything to go by. In 1947, at the time of Independence, the population of India was 370 million, but in under 40 years it has doubled. It is a fair guess that the next 15 years or so will see another 300 million Indians born who will survive, and by AD 2000 India will somehow have to absorb its 1000 million.

It is a very worrying problem for India and for the rest of the world, and a very far cry from the ancient days of the Harappans and the Dravidians and the Aryan invasion . . .

Languages

The States of India can be likened to the countries of Europe, each of which has its own language. It is useful when travelling around India to remember that, as when travelling across Europe, one is really passing from one country to another – the 'country' in India being called a State. The State of Rajasthan, for instance, is nearly as large as the country of France. As one passes from State to State, so the languages change. The inter-State linguistic bond is either Hindi, the first language of India, or English, the second language.

There are 14 major languages spoken in India, and around 250 regional dialects. Other than English, the most widespread language is Hindi. This language is spoken by an estimated half of the population, most of whom live in northern India.

The languages of the south of India, the Dravidian languages, are very different. The four main ones are Telegu, spoken throughout Andhra Pradesh; Kanada, spoken throughout Karnataka; Tamil, spoken throughout Tamil Nadu, and Malayalam, the main language of Kerala. These languages have little in common with Hindi other than some Sanskrit origins, and each has its own script, as indeed do northern Indian languages – Gujarati and Haryanwi being slightly different from the Devanagari script of Hindi, and Bengali being quite different.

The Inter-State boundaries were created originally with a view to uniting peoples of similar languages and dialects under a common administration. English is widely used throughout the south, especially for official and commercial purposes. State legislation may opt for any of the languages listed in the Indian Constitution.

Hindi is the official language of the Union of the States of India. The general policy of the Government is to encourage progressive use of Hindi as the official language, but English continues to be used alongside or in addition to Hindi for most official purposes of Union (Central) Government and for communication between States; and also for the transaction of business in Parliament.

The use of English as a second language throughout India is a well-debated subject which is constantly being aired in articles and letters published by the national and State presses. English – to be spoken or not to be spoken – provokes patriotic outbursts the year round and though most arguments for and against the use of English have some validity, this is usually within the circumscribed viewpoints of the writers, be they personal or political. Whatever the objections, the fact remains that English is a common bonding language throughout India, just as it has been for years throughout Europe.

The States and their peoples

Who are the peoples who make up India? Indians? In a general way, yes,

States and union territories: their capitals and languages

State	Capital	Main Language	Other language
Andhra Pradesh	Hyderabad	Telegu	
Assam	Gauhati	Assamese	Bengali
Bihar	Patna	Hindi	
Gujarat	Gandhinagar	Gujarati	
Harayana	Chandigarh	Hindi	
Himachal Pradesh	Simla	Hindi	Pahari
Jammu & Kashmir	Srinagar (summer) Jammu (winter)	Kashmiri	Dogri
Karnataka	Bangalore	Kanada	
Kerala	Trivandrum	Malayalam	
Madhya Pradesh	Bhopal	Hindi	
Maharastra	Bombay	Marati	
Manipur	Imphal	Manipuri	
Meghalaya	Shillong	Khasi	Garo
Nagaland	Kohima	Naganese	English
Orissa	Bhubaneswar	Orya	
Punjab	Chandigarh	Punjabi	
Rajasthan	Jaipur	Rajasthani	
Sikkim	Gantok	Nepali	Bhutia
Tamil Nadu	Madras	Tamil	
Tripura	Agartala	Assamese	Bengali
Uttar Pradesh	Lucknow	Hindi	Urdu
West Bengal	Calcutta	Bengali	

Union territories

State	Capital	Main Language	Other language
Andaman & Nicobar Islands	Port Blair	English	Tribal
Arunachal Pradesh	Itanagar	Assamese	
Chandigarh	(State capital)	Punjabi	Hindi
New Delhi	(National capital)	Hindi	Urdu
Goa, Daman, Diu	Panaji	Marathi	Konkani
Lakshadweep Is.	Karawathy	Tribal	English
Mizoram	Aizawal	Tribal Mizo	English
Pondicherry	(State capital)	Tamil	French

but in particular, and in the words of Jawaharlal Nehru, India's first Prime Minister and grandfather of the present Prime Minister, Rajiv Gandhi, 'There is no such thing as an Indian. One is either (say) a Punjabi, a Gujarati, a Tamil or a Kashmiri, and then an Indian'.

This remark has a ring of truth about it. Leaving aside the wider national aspect of India, and thinking more of cultural aspects, of the sophisticated element, of politics, newspapers, magazines, schools, the army or the police, the vastness of India is mostly village India.

The villager in the heart of Bihar may be a supporter of the Congress Party and therefore be voting in an election as an Indian, but he will think of himself first as a Bihari. Most people in Gujarat think of themselves as Gujaratis; they are Gujarati first and Indian second. That all peoples are Indian as of nationality binds the web of national responsibility, helping the Indian Government to keep its country under control, and secure.

Separatism within India is a very real thing and never more so than at present. Literacy has brought with it agitators who cause unrest where once there was 'the uneasy quiet'. One has only to hear the Tamils of the south talking about their 'own language', Tamil, the oldest language in the world; of their culture and independence as a State in all the natural resources, to understand that these feelings run very deep. With its own State Government, Tamil Nadu is nevertheless subject to ultimate rule from Delhi; there rests the final power. Some Sikhs, too, want a separate State and there have been ugly demonstrations in recent years in order to try and force the Central Government to create some form of autonomy in the Punjab.

It is most improbable that a villager in, say, Karnataka, toiling on his land, coping with the seasons, arranging the marriages of his children, observing the festivals of his land and the predictions of the priest, would ever come to know his Bengali 'Indian brother', who is himself going about a similar routine in his life, but both may have voted for the same political party in a general election and both would fight for India, their country, yet neither speaks the other's language and they live over 1609 km (1000 miles) apart!

One can understand what Jawaharlal Nehru meant, therefore, when he said that there was no such thing as an Indian. The people of India are all very different individuals and it is useful and illuminating for a visitor to know a little about these differences; it can explain many things that might perplex a traveller, and unravel some of the reasons as to why people act as they do.

In a very general way, though, and taking India from north to south, first comes the State of Jammu and Kashmir, where the people are known mostly by the term 'Kashmiris'. They are fair and have aquiline faces, large noses, and tend to be tall. They are predominantly Muslim but there are quite large Hindu and Christian communities living in the State. 'Kept fair by the snows', I was once told by a Kashmiri by way of explaining their paleness, 'Here we are nearer to our Gods.' He was a Hindu.

Below Jammu and Kashmir are the States of Punjab, Haryana, Himachal Pradesh and the city and capital State of Delhi. The Punjab is the home of both the Sikhs and the Punjabis. Because of the waters from rivers such as the Sutlej and the Beas and the Jumna, this area is very fertile and wheat is grown abundantly, earning the State of Punjab the epithet 'The granary of India'. The people of Haryana speak Haryanwi, which is similar to Hindi, and in Himachal Pradesh they speak a variety of hill dialects, Hindi and English, the latter being picked up in a variety of forms from the wandering 'hippies' who proliferate here when it is getting too hot in places such as Goa or Cochin. In the Punjab the village farmer predominates and he is never very far from being relatively wealthy. The Sikhs, too, are fine business entrepreneurs; many are drivers and many work in the motor industry, and almost all the Delhi taxi drivers seem to be Sikhs. In Haryana farming and husbandry take precedence, whilst Himachal Pradesh relies on its tourism, both from the pilgrim Indian and the annual appearance of footloose American, Australian and European 'back-packers'. Relatively few visitors travel to Simla, the most famous of the northern hill stations. Other than travellers and the back-pack brigade, Simla seems to have been overlooked, or not considered; most tourists seem to fly over it, en route to Kashmir.

Towards the south, India begins to spread from west to east, and as the rivers which nourish the Punjab and make it India's granary flow off into neighbouring Pakistan, one comes to Rajasthan – country of kings, of desert and of a very different-looking people. This is a country of Rajput warriors, Rajput clans, fighting men who have attenuated features, dark or light according to their genealogy. Rajasthan is a dry area which can be inhospitable to the Rajasthani, let alone to the visitor. It has extremes of temperature, going from icy cold to baking hot. The people speak regional dialects which, combined with Hindustani, loosely make up the Rajasthani spoken throughout the State today.

From Rajasthan eastwards is Uttar Pradesh, a vast tract of land containing almost the whole of the Gangetic Plain. Populated largely by Muslims up until Independence, and still predominantly Muslim in many areas, the people here live by agriculture and by industrial development. They are somewhat darker in appearance than the Rajasthani, are a mixture of cultures, are hot-blooded, are given to communalism and accustomed to seeing the Westerner only in the main 'tourist' places – as far apart as Agra with the Taj Mahal and Benares with the River Ganges.

Bihar is a State seldom visited by foreigners, though it is crossed in the journey from east to west. Here there is the ruined university complex at Nalanda, and, nearby, Bodh Gaya, where the Lord Buddha attained enlightenment (under the bo tree); but, apart from saffron clad wanderers, Western visitors are few. This has long been a backward and lawless area of India. The horrific Bhagalpur blindings have not been forgotten, and atrocities such as this are still perpetrated today. It is bandit territory, too, and there is a lot of smuggling to and from Nepal, with which Bihar has its northern border.

3 Udaipur Lake Palace – sumptuous architectural jewel of Rajasthan

4 The ruins of Nalanda – Bihar

'We have to keep loaded guns behind our doors', a fellow traveller told me. I asked why it was necessary.

'You see, we fear those from Nepal.'

'But the Nepalis are a peaceful people.'

'It's not the Nepalis we fear, it is our own smugglers.'

'What is smuggled?'

'All sorts of things. When we are short of food, then it is food, foreign food, not Nepali food; from Hong Kong, Germany, in tins. Also radios and cameras and drink and drugs. We never know.'

'Why the gun – would you shoot a smuggler?'

'No, it is like this. It may be in the middle of the night, you see, there will be banging on the door. We have to open, it may be the police, but often it is the smuggler. He threatens us that if we do not hide the goods he has until the police no longer want him, then he will kill one of us, or burn our home. He would, too. It has happened for many years now, it goes on. Now we have a hiding place. The police know about it but we can pay them, they take bribes. We even hide the smuggler at times. All people do that; it is the custom and the gun is our protection from the evil of everyone.'

'You keep it behind the door?'

'Yes, to protect the smuggler and his property.' He saw me smile. 'It is true. Others will tell you the same. People will come, strangers will come and they will demand that we given them some goods, a radio or something. It is hard. Some even have to shoot.'

'Have you ever had to fire your gun?'

'I have, but not to kill.'

Any doubts about the veracity of this story were dispelled by spending more time and meeting more people in the region: protectionism and fear do go hand in hand with smuggling.

The urbanized people of West Bengal tend to be of small stature, to have round faces and to be very gregarious and Western. In the north of the State there is Darjeeling, a quiet and peaceful place among the mountains, with transcendental views and a mixture of hill people, Assamese, British and Bengalis.

Beyond and to the east of West Bengal, beyond what is now Bangladesh, lies Assam and its mongoloid-featured peoples, its British residents, its tea growers (now almost all Assamese), its tribals and its fearful refugee problem. Running down its middle is the mighty Bramhaputra river, a life-line or a danger, depending on the season of the year. Nearby live the Nagas, once noted as 'living naked to their skins', but now mostly clothed. They are actually descendants of the original tribals who populated northern India together with communities of Dravidians before the Aryan invasion.

India here, from east to west, is at its widest and is very full of wonders. Southwards, one comes to Gujarat, Madhya Pradesh (the area once known as Central Provinces), Orissa and Maharashtra.

The people of Gujarat have long since made the world their home. They have travelled throughout Africa, Australia, America and Britain and have successfully settled and prospered. Fair-skinned, and of less than average height they are excellent businessmen and seem mostly to be called Patel! It is said that they, together with the Brahmins, control the riches of modern India, a notable Patel success being the Patel Motels in America.

Other than Bombay and Poona, Madhya Pradesh and Maharashtra are quiet areas of India. Not many tourists (as opposed to travellers) stray very far in these States. Here are industries such as coal mining, iron ore mines and electricity generating that mingle with, or fight with, jungle and famine. Madhya Pradesh does not have a sea coast, its huge size lying within central India like an enormous heart. There are many Bhil and Gond tribals among the hills and jungles. Dacoity (robbery with violence) is rife in this difficult-of-access area. There are, however, many beauties that persuade a traveller to visit here, of which Gwalior, Khajuraho, Shivpuri, Mandu, Indore and Bhopal are but some.

East, in Orissa, where the Indian coast runs from Calcutta southwards, the name which springs to mind most readily is Konarak and the Sun Temple. This comparatively small State has more than the obvious to enchant and interest. The Orayans are a friendly and gentle people: many follow Buddha, and fishing is very much a part of the economy of the State. It is a land of green fields and of village life, of holiday places by the sea, like Lake Chilka, much of it undeveloped yet with amenities for those who are prepared to seek them out.

Below and south of these masses of India are the four southern States of Karnataka, Andhra Pradesh, Kerala and Tamil Nadu, together with the small enclaves of Portuguese Goa, Daman and French Pondicherry, now ceded as Union Territories within India.

Karnataka was formerly known as Mysore State and is now home for many Europeans. Bangalore is its cultural centre and there English, French, Germans, Americans and, not surprisingly, Indians, enjoy life. Bangalore has a delightful climate all the year round. The language is Kanada, with some Konkani and English.

Tamil is the oldest language in the world, impossible to learn, and a Tamilian would not expect you to master his language, though he would be delighted if you uttered a few words. English has long been spoken (missionary influence) by all Tamil Nadu's dark-skinned people. The State is a wonderland of things to see and is very much developed by the local Tourist Development Corporation; in fact, all the south seems to lead in this respect. One should remember that there are thousands more Indian travellers travelling around India than ever there are foreigners and it is partly to cater for them that so much has been done by way of hotel comfort and other facilities.

Westwards in Kerala, the State which runs down the west coast of India like a banana, Christianity is more in evidence. This area of India

5 One of the massive carved wheels of the Sun Temple – Konarak

6 Fisherman mending his net in front of the Fort of Portuguese Daman

7 Silver Sands Beach leading to Mahabalipuram in Tamil Nadu

has always been most tolerant of differing religions and this intermingling shows on the faces of many Keralites. Many have strongly European characteristics. It is a highly literate State, the literacy rate being 60 per cent, or twice the all-India average, and, as mentioned elsewhere, 'exports' a lot of its talent. The State is, alas, vastly over-populated and therefore impoverished, and though the remedy is obvious, the mixture of Catholic and Hindu traditions is a certain recipe for too many children.

In spite of this, Kerala is a beautiful place and has more than its fair share of happy faces, a feature, incidentally, to be seen all over India where poverty is the order of the day.

Government, the States and politics

India is the world's largest democracy. Its governmental system could be described as a mixture, an adaptation, of British and American procedures, though in no sense is it a copy of either.

The head of the country is the President and to advise him there exists a Council of Ministers responsible to the Lok Sabha, the House of the People, similar to the House of Commons in Britain. The President's term of office is five years, as is that of the British Prime Minister.

The constitution of the Union of States that forms India provides for a system of parliamentary and cabinet government, both central (from Delhi) and within each of the States. This is where the American plan is echoed, in that, in the USA the people have central government and federal control throughout the States. In Britain, the parallel is not so obvious, as the local government, for example at county level, is very different from that in the States of either America or India.

The Central Government of India represents the interests of all the States as a Union, the country as a whole, in fact, whereas State government represents local interests. The Indian States have their own hierarchy of command headed by the Governor, who is appointed by the President of India, not the Prime Minister, as may be expected. In central government the Prime Minister is at the head of the ladder of command.

Politically, India is altogether a country apart from the West. Although she has many Western aspects, outlooks and allegiances, India is very much an Eastern country and must represent the majority of its peoples, 80 per cent of whom live in villages in the rural heartlands, where 83 per cent of them are Hindu. Effective control through the Indian Parliament depends very much on the rural vote.

In these rural areas there is a form of local government known as the panchayat system (see Village India).

The Indian Constitution provides for a uniform citizenship for the whole of India. All persons born in India, or whose parents were born in India, are citizens and all are entitled to vote from the age of 21.

India has an independent judiciary. The Supreme Court, consisting of a Chief Justice and 17 judges appointed by the President, is the final arbiter on constitutional matters. It exercises exclusive jurisdiction on any dispute between the Union (Central) Government and a State, or between States themselves. There is a High Court in each State. Courts of Session and Courts of Magistrates have jurisdiction in criminal cases, and District Courts deal with civil cases. At the village level the panchayat, or village court, tries minor offences both of a criminal and of a civic nature. Their powers of punishment are limited to the imposition of fines – a valuable weapon, or control, amongst a largely poor people.

The present-day political ideologies that exist in India are, in the main, pies in the Indian sky. The chances of bringing about a cohesion of aims between the members of one political party alone are slim indeed. This makes it far easier for the powers that be to preach what they can never practise. The waters of modern political actions over which the huge populace may be said to float have suffered a sea-change from a democracy to a democratic autocracy which was, until 1984, led, commanded, bullied, bamboozled and mothered by the redoubtable and much respected Mrs Indira Gandhi.

Only once in her long political leadership did Mrs Gandhi lose the majority vote and this was due to facts which have become legendary in modern Indian history. The excesses of the Emergency measures taken between 1975–7, imposed by her and carried out by, amongst many, her son, Sanjay Gandhi, need no recitation here.

During her long term out of office, when the country was run by an ineffective opposition, Mrs Gandhi, when either in prison or under house arrest, wielded such influence throughout the country that she remained its effective, though unofficial, leader.

Mrs Gandhi's personal triumph, sweeping back to power in 1977, put her once again in full command. Overcoming the death of her much loved, but somewhat contentious, first son, Sanjay, she introduced her second son, Rajiv, into the Congress (I) Party's machinery. After her assassination, Rajiv Gandhi was declared Prime Minister, going on to win an overwhelming majority for the party in the December 1984 general election.

The five-year plans introduced by successive governments run by the Congress Party have ensured a steady development in community care, food distribution, irrigation, literacy and the consolidation of India as a power that is dominant throughout Central Asia. India has been seen to be as reliable as every other similar power and now has command of her own satellite – is, in fact, a space-age nation.

What, though, are the aspirations of the parties? To all intents and purposes there is little opposition to the Congress Party's lead. Congress (I), as it is known, has a right-wing outlook with an open attitude to foreign policy, which benefits India's position as a power throughout the world. The Janata Party set out to appeal directly to the massive rural vote, concentrating more on development of farming, because so many of the people of India are in some way or another farmers or landowners.

Though the Janata Party's politicians are less clear about their policies, they have a definite following but never a lasting majority. In Parliament, though, any opposition can pose problems and frequently and successfully oppose bills and obstruct Parliament's intentions.

The Communist Party, long established in the south in Kerala, though much less so following the 1984 general election, is also effective elsewhere – notably in West Bengal, where its majority was also reduced. It is doubtful if within India as a whole, it will ever gain any ascendancy over the main parties.

There will always be such things as communal disturbances in a country with so many differing peoples, races and religions, but the Hindu majority is basically a following race – they like to be led, and feel secure in being told what to do.

India's internal problems are immense and, in wrestling with them, any government must consider both national and international opinion. This is not an easy task when one considers that all aspects of the Union and the State governments and the people who are governed have Eastern ideas, Eastern morals and Eastern culture – characteristics that have been welded by 4000 years of civilization, by wars, by rule, but, most of all, by being Oriental.

Village India

Out of a population of approximately 700 million Indians, 80 per cent live, as mentioned, in villages. This village population, of which only roughly a third is literate, is nevertheless articulate and constitutes a great source of voting power and economical strength.

There are few Indians who do not have village roots or some land somewhere and, though they may work and live in town or city, this land sustains their feeling of belonging to India – a feeling that no concrete jungle could provoke.

Most Indians who work away from home will return to their village, no matter how far they have travelled or how successful they have become.

A typical, average, village that has been the nucleus of a community for hundreds of years will consist of a cluster of mud huts with, perhaps, one or two concrete houses from which will jut concrete balconies, probably painted green or pink. In these houses live the more prosperous families. The village will be surrounded by fields interlaced by narrow dust pathways and wide earth cart-tracks. During the monsoon season a 'nullah', or small stream, might run through and will irrigate the land. The bullock will be more in evidence than the tractor, and female labour more to be seen than that of the menfolk.

Whatever the condition of the village, life is always a struggle. If the village is a poor one, then the struggle is mainly to survive; if prosperous, then the struggle will be to remain prosperous. A further burden are the taxes demanded by the government from all.

Some villages are Hindu, some are Muslim; others are Christian, and there are Harijan villages too. One would need to be very familiar with everyday life in rural India to confidently tell the difference, though some clues would be obvious. The Christian church, for instance, or the Hindu temple or the Muslim mosque – each would proclaim the identity of a particular village. In the smaller villages there would be no such evidence. Also, there are mixed communities living in one village; the pattern is very confusing, but it works and it forms the backbone of India.

In the Indian village one might expect to see only the basic necessities of life, but included in these will be the transistor radio, the cassette player and even, more and more, the television. Communication by TV to the masses is well under way and constitutes a 'miracle' for the people. One can only conjecture at the political power that village television will have in the future.

If you receive an invitation to visit or to stay in an Indian village then accept it, as it will be an unusual and happy experience. Wherever you go in India, hospitality is generously given and nowhere more so than in a village, no matter how poor.

There will almost always be something to celebrate (apart from your arrival!) and you will be included in whatever is happening. It may be a celebration to honour some local deity or to mark a festival or a betrothal, or to attend a marriage ceremony. Life revolves very much around birth, marriage, death and cultivation.

The village wakes before dawn, when the air is cool. Then the farmers go out to the fields and complete a day's work before midday, resting during the afternoon and returning to the fields when the daytime heat has abated, to work until dusk.

The children of the village are doted on by both their parents and their grandparents. They are the focus of the community and are given all freedom, until about seven years old. Then they will start to work, tending goats or the cows or running errands. This way they learn the ways of the village and the land. Some will be educated in the village school, under one of the spreading neem trees. Others, more fortunate, will go off to a Government school, whilst very few will be sent, by prosperous parents, to a boarding school. Most, though, will fall into the rural cycle, resigned to a life of toil.

There is a high standard of morality in rural India, morality in the social sense. Indian sexuality is no more or less intense than in other countries. When one considers the vast extent of Indian village life, communal strife is a relatively infrequent happening. When it does break out, it makes headlines in the Indian newspapers. Hindus and Muslims live mostly in harmony, venerating each other's tombs and shrines. They often consult the same astrologer, yet discord is always lurking beneath the surface and it takes only the smallest thing to spark off the most frightful violence.

Astrology very much influences the Indian mind, and most Indians

8 Village cattle boy sits beneath an ancient pipal tree

consult one on matters like marriage or money. They seem to wish to be given confidence in how to act: how to marry their daughter, when to sow their crops, when to make a pilgrimage, when to invest money. In fact, they will consult the astrologer before most activities and especially before naming the baby. Astrology is not a superstition, it is a belief in an ancient science which has been proved more often correct than not, and astrological advice is sought throughout India, from the rulers to the ruled.

The priest, too, plays an important part in village life. He intercedes between the gods and man very directly. He has power in the village, often taking the place of lawyer, counsellor and sometimes judge. For his services he makes a charge and on this income he and his temple exist. The village priest will usually be married with several children.

The village panchayat is a concise example of government by the people, of the people, for the people. This body of locally elected men runs all the affairs connected with the civic workings of the village. Land

9 A water-village near Quillon in Kerala

allotment, dowry, water supply, sanitation, drainage, road building, planting, and relations with other villages are a few of the responsibilities of the panchayat. These responsibilities differ from north to south but eventually the panchayat will be responsible to the State government.

The passing visitor should try not to evaluate what he sees of an Indian village in Western terms but rather try to imagine the life there and understand something of what goes to making village life. The mud wall, the dust road, the mangy dog, the unwashed children and the careworn womenfolk, the lean cattle and dried cow-dung are all meaningful within the context of an Indian village. They seem to be ancient and inevitable.

One finds that, where betterment has come to a village community, the evidence will not be obvious. One has to look deeper – for signs of well-fed children, more cattle, more land divisions, irrigation and a tractor. The village will not wear its prosperity on its sleeve by painting its houses and trimming its hedges or by metalling its roads, but it may send a son to university or have relatives working in a city, even across the waters in one of the Gulf States.

Because of traditions, the climate, superstitions, fear, resignation and over-population, village life will always be a harsh one but it is, by its enormity, the backbone of India and the cradle of India's ancient culture.

When travelling across India, village life cannot be disregarded. One sees it from the train window, the coach window and even from the air through the plane window. It represents a pattern which stretches back in time for centuries and will continue to dominate the thoughts and ways of India no matter how modern the outside world.

11 Religion

Hinduism

Hinduism was not founded by any one sage or teacher in the way that, for instance, Christianity was founded by Jesus Christ, or Islam by the Prophet Mohammed, neither was it planned in the socio-political sense as a means of public control or order. It grew out of the ancient Vedic scriptures, interpreted by an early intellectual, Manu. He translated the meanings of Vedism (the worship of nature) into a domestic code that would be understood by the people, and he created the four principal castes in Hindu society. This division of the populace proved to be a religious and a social control that has lasted throughout the years. From these divisions sprang the way of life that is loosely called Hinduism. The legends are so interwoven throughout a Hindu's life that they have become fact and are now very real beliefs.

Over 80 per cent of India's population is Hindu. A Hindu believes in one God, but through many manifestations. It may be through Lord Krishna, or Lord Shiva, or Lord Vishnu, or be an admixture of all the vast pantheon of gods, of which there are many thousands. In the temples will be found deities represented in the form of the many mythological characters in the great Hindu epics such as the Mahabharata. (Incidentally, this is the longest poem ever written, containing over three million words.) The heart of the Mahabharata is the Bhagavad Gita, or Sacred Song. There are, too, the Upanishads; the Sanskrit verses called the *Puranas*; and the marvellous story of the Ramayana. It is within these writings that the beliefs of Hinduism can be found. Hinduism is based on the idea that each individual will go through a progression of rebirths that eventually lead to a spiritual salvation which frees him from this cycle and leads to Nirvanah. Bad actions in life can lead to a lower reincarnation and, conversely, good actions to a higher reincarnation. The way a person behaves in life is called Karma. Karma is, therefore, self-controlled. The other daily factor of Hinduism, Dharma, is the inevitable by which man is controlled, i.e. by natural laws, by the universe, by his caste, which is irrevocable, and by a moral code that is inherent. A Hindu practises three basics: puja (worship), the burning of the dead and the observance of caste. The Hindu does not proselytize and no one not born a Hindu can become one.

The principal caste in Hinduism, the highest, is the Brahmin or priest caste, followed by the Kshastrias, the warriors, fighters or governors. Then come the Vaisayas, the farmers, craftsmen and tradesmen, and after them the Sudras, who do the manual or physical work, like labouring. The people who have no caste were once called Untouchables. Now, though, they are referred to as Harijans, or Children of God, as Mahatma Gandhi called them, and they do all the menial and dirty work.

Casteism has not changed since Independence. After thousands of years it will take much longer to eradicate this social separating, and one questions whether or not Hindu India could survive without caste.

The principal deities of Hinduism are:

Brahma, the Creator. He has four heads from which sprang the Vedas, the early scriptures. He is considered to be the god of wisdom.

Saraswati, Brahma's wife. She is depicted riding on a swan and is the goddess of learning.

Shiva is worshipped in the form of a lingam, a phallic symbol, most frequently found in a Shiva temple. He is known as the destroyer.

Parvati, Shiva's wife, the interceder.

Nandi, the bull. The bull was Shiva's mount and is always seen in a Shiva temple.

Ganesh, the elephant-headed son of Shiva. He is thought to bring good luck and is often worshipped before undertaking new enterprises.

Vishnu, the preserver. The second most important Hindu god, he appears incarnated as Krishna and as Rama, the hero of the epic Ramayana. Krishna is the god of love. His childhood, adolescence and manhood are recounted in the Bhagavad Gita.

Lakshmi, the wife of Vishnu. Often depicted seated on a lotus, she represents wealth and prosperity and is represented in one incarnation as Sita, the wife of Rama.

10 Foot of 'the 1001' steps leading uphill past shrines to the Chaumundi Temple, Mysore

11 · Mythological figures – Sacra, one of the names of the god Indra, visiting the Buddha – seen left

Garuda, Vishnu's mount. This is a large bird with the body of a man and the head of an eagle.

These deities, in one manifestation or another, will be found throughout India in temples, on civic architecture, on wayside shrines, on the summit of any high ground, in the home, on the classical stage in the form of dance and song and, by no means least, in modern India, on the cinema screen.

Hinduism is, therefore, a way of life, bound by ancient beliefs in mythology, and it contains the tenets by which the Hindu lives, the disciplines that organize his family life, his feelings about nature, about sexuality, about birth and death, and about life after death. It is a wholeness that satisfies the masses individually; it has no dogma and no rule for all. It is very personal and to those who are not Hindu it presents an attractive pattern for a spiritual life.

Islam

The Islamic religion came comparatively late into India, but from AD 1000 it gradually gained ground, either by self-generation or by voluntary or compulsory conversion. After the Emperor Babur had vanquished the Sultans of Delhi – the 'Delhi Moghuls' – and had founded the beginning of the Moghul Empire, then began the 'Golden Age of Islam' in India.

The founder of the Islamic religion was the Prophet Mohammed. He was born at Mecca, in what is now Saudi Arabia, in AD 570, of a family of the Quaraish tribe. The child was something of a marvel. Being orphaned whilst only six years old, his grandfather took over his care. When Mohammed was twelve he accompanied his grandfather on a journey to Syria. The story goes, and there is no reason to disbelieve it, that half way there, on staying with a Christian monk named Bahira, the monk exclaimed that there was 'a cloud following you and it has stopped over your caravan'. The monk then examined the body of Mohammed and discovered the mark of prophethood between the boy's shoulder-blades. The monk counselled immediate return to Mecca, fearing that harm might come to Mohammed, advice upon which his grandfather acted.

From the time of his return to Mecca, Mohammed's reputation for being trustworthy, honest and wise increased. Some time afterwards he did go to Syria, this time at the behest of a wealthy merchant's widow called Khadija. She said that if he would take care of her goods she would pay him more liberally than had others, and he returned successful, having made much profit for the widow. She was so delighted that she sent Mohammed a proposal of marriage. He accepted and they were married, he being 25 and she 40 years old.

More and more his spiritual nature necessitated his going alone into the desert to meditate. It was on one of these lonely occasions that the Angel Gabriel spoke to him about a new religion and bade him write down his message that came direct from God. This first revelation happened when Mohammed was 40 years old, in AD 610. Later, the Qur'an, or Koran as it is known in the West, was gradually revealed to him in simple sentences or paragraphs, from which he began to teach the new religion.

Mohammed was recognized as a prophet and he preached the beginnings of a faith which was to become all-powerful throughout Asia. He died, aged 62, in Medina, the city after Mecca that is most sacred to Islam.

A Muslim must believe in one God, in good and evil, and in a fate and a life after death. The Muslim faith, then full of zeal and a new awareness, was more than a religion which people could follow; it called upon them to spread the word, by force if necessary, and many were those who accepted the Islamic way rather than die.

Islam's spread throughout the West was checked by Christianity (with which, oddly, it has much in common) in mid-France. Eastwards its influence waxed so strong that eventually Muslim dhows invaded India via the Indus; it was then AD 711.

There are no actual priests in Mohammedism but in practice each mosque will be found to have in charge of it a Mullah – a fairly powerful figure in the community, as witnessed in present-day Iran. Everyone is his own priest in charge of his own spirituality, and this makes fanaticism never far below the surface. Muslims believe that each person is respon-sible for his own actions and will answer for them on the Day of

Judgment. The whole life of a Muslim is, or should be, dedicated to the worship of God. The compulsory duties of a Muslim are to say prayers five times a day, to give alms, to fast in the month of Ramadan and to make a pilgrimage to Mecca once during his lifetime. Before prayers he must wash the hands with pure water up to the wrists three times; he must rinse out the mouth and cleanse the nose by rinsing and also wash both arms up to the elbows three times. Finally, he must wash his feet three times. It is not surprising, therefore, that one sees water pools and running taps adjacent to all mosques. After such ablutions, the faithful can worship according to the tenets of the Holy Koran. The Koran contains 114 chapters which themselves contain 6,200 verses; and there is no doubt as to its historical authenticity. Mohammed appointed learned writers to set down exactly the revelations he received.

Mohammedans believe that to worship God through images such as idols or any representation of the human form is blasphemous. It is this belief more than any other that brought about the desecration of most Hindu architecture during Muslim rule over India.

The Islamic calendar is based on the lunar system and the months determined by the appearance of the new moon. This dating began after Mohammed had moved from Mecca to Medina, 482 km (300 miles) distant. The year 1985, therefore, in the Islamic calendar would be 1405 AH – After Hiraj – the name given to Mohammed's migration to Medina.

There are four great religious occasions in the Islamic Year. The most well known to Westerners is Muharram, which happens during February. This festival remembers Hussain, Mohammed's grandson, the son of Ali by Fatima, who was the daughter of Mohammed. A period of fasting is followed by a procession in which each community of Muslims in the area (and they can be many in the cities of India) carries a representation of the tomb of Hussain. These are called 'tazia' and are several feet high, made of a light wooden construction which is covered in tissue paper and tinsel and coloured stripes in the form of a domed and minaretted building; much like a small Taj Mahal. The 'tazias' are taken to the most convenient water, either a river or a lake, and are immersed to prayers and chanting. Fervour runs high at this time and it takes only a small incident to spark off trouble.

The festival of Bakr Id, in January, is in memory of Abraham offering to sacrifice his son, Ishmael – a story related in the Koran. On this occasion goats or other animals are sacrificed.

Ramadan, October time, is a month-long festival when continuous daily fasting is observed. Neither food nor drink may be taken between sunrise and sunset. Because of the lunar calendar it is a movable feast. At the end of Ramadan there is the festival of Id-ul-fitr, when fasting is over and feasting begins.

Buddhism

It is generally accepted that the Buddha was born in 624 BC and died in

544 BC. Buddha's name was Siddharta Gautama, two names heard often in India as names for a son; or even a hotel! Gautama changed his name to that of Buddha afer receiving enlightenment from God. Buddha means 'The Enlightened One'.

Renouncing all worldly things and all worldly pleasures at the age of 29, Buddha left home and his wife, whom he had married at the age of 16, and, with his hair cut off, and poorly dressed, he joined two holy men. They were two Brahmin priests and he wished to observe their life and practise their austerities. The rigours of this new life were heightened by the fact that he came from a wealthy family and was used to all the comforts and privilege that come from belonging to such a family.

He was tormented by memories of the indulgent living of others whilst so many had so little, and he was determined to find a means of relieving the suffering of less privileged people.

At the age of 25, when he was sitting under a bo tree on the banks of the river Niranjara near Gaya, in the present-day State of Bihar, enlightenment came to him from God, a momentous happening for him, and his future at once became clear.

He became known as Buddha, the one who is awakened to the truth,

12 Lord Buddha

and he immediately began to preach his way of life – the way that had been revealed to him when meditating.

He preached his first sermon at Sarnath, 6 km (4 miles) from Varanasi (Benares). He told his listeners stories and parables much in the same way as did Jesus Christ, and soon attracted a large following.

He called the way of life 'The Middle Way', a kind of centre course between the asceticism of the monastery and the indulgence of life without any control, and he soon had a group of disciples around him. Life for this community developed a new meaning and its members went off on travels preaching 'The Middle Way'.

There were no social degrees, all men were (and are) equal on becoming a part of Buddhism. One automatically sheds material values, or the lack of them, and becomes only a follower of Buddha.

The Buddha died at the age of 80, which was a good age for the times. He attained Nirvanah, being free from the cycles of rebirth. After cremation of his body its remains were divided amongst several of his followers and each part was thereinafter enshrined in a holy mound, called a 'stupa' – a domed mound.

In India, Buddhism developed swiftly and not the least because the Emperor Asoka embraced the Buddha's teachings. Asoka's empire extended everywhere except to the south of India. In the north the spread of Buddhism was assured. Asoka erected huge pillars of stone wherever he went and he had written on them the virtues of Buddhism. These 'Edicts of Asoka' were his personal law, a law based upon or inspired by the teachings of Buddha. One such pillar is to be seen at Sarnath. On the top of this pillar once stood the four-headed lion that is now the national symbol of India.

13 Votive stupas at Bodh Gaya

Buddhism is important in India if for no other reason than that it was first conceived there. The only other religions founded in India are Hinduism, Jainism and, much later, Sikhism. There are about five million Buddhists throughout India, an oddly small number when compared with the population of 700 million. One reason may be that to convert to Buddhism requires a great deal of self-discipline, something that, as with other races of people, many Hindus lack; especially in the more materialistic purlieus of the middle classes.

Jainism

At the time Alexander invaded north-west India (526/7 BC), Mahavira, the founder of Jainism, died. He was 70 years old.

He was born near Patna, the son of a ruling family, and, until his late twenties, was content with his privileged position. Then, much like Siddharta Gautama, the founder of Buddhism, Mahavira became dissatisfied with material life and, aged 30, entered a monastery as a monk of the Parsanavatha order.

By the time he was 40 he had reached a state of spirituality, so much so that it was recognized that he had rare gifts for divination and leadership.

He foresook his family name of Vardhamana and took the title Mahavira, 'divine conqueror', then called a Jina. It is from the word 'Jina' that Jainism is derived.

Jainism is divided into two sects, the Svetambras and the Digambras. The former wear either white or saffron cloth, the latter do not wear anything – the strict members that is. There are many Digambra Jains who are worldly and go about their business in an ordinary way and are not recognizable in the community.

The Jains did not cut themselves off from Hinduism, and many priests in their temples are Brahmins. Jains, like Buddhists, believe in the Hindu pantheon of gods, but all Jains are stringent vegetarians.

Jains are mostly found over the north-western area of India and it is there that their great temple complexes can be seen. Palitana is one such, only a quick flight from Bombay. Mount Abu, in southern Rajasthan (a night journey by train from Jaipur or Bombay) is where the famous Dilwara Jain temples are, perhaps the most fabulous examples of Jain architecture. Mount Abu is also a charming hill station with walks and climbs and boating and is a good detour to make if time permits.

On the whole, Jains are intelligent and successful people who wield much social influence for good, especially among local communities. Most of them live as a communal family, needing large houses, yet there is rarely any sign of ostentation. Indeed, to the Western eye their life would seem to be a spartan one, but they enjoy comforts, entertainment, fine clothes and gold, only in a relatively quiet way.

Sikhism

Guru Nanak, the founder of the Sikh religion, was born in 1469. He was a member of the caste known as Kshastrias – those who, according to the Laws of Manu (see Caste), were allowed to learn the Vedas but could not become a religious teacher or a priest. The caste system had become inflexible and oppressive by the fifteenth century; from the cradle to the grave one was compelled to live within one's caste. Guru Nanak was not alone in opposing the caste system, but he was powerful enough as a personality actually to become a religious teacher; and he rejected the Vedas, taught in the local dialects of his people and accepted disciples from amongst them irrespective of caste. He insisted that all should eat from the same dish, a revolutionary step then and rejected even now by the strict Brahmins of today.

Guru Nanak was born at Talwandi, a medium-sized village some 64 km (40 miles) south-west of Lahore, now in Pakistan. Throughout his life he tried to unite the Hindu and the Muslim and all the many religions then practised in India, so that at least they would understand their differences. For 20 years he travelled with a Muslim poet, Mardana, as his companion as far as Ceylon and Tibet and to Mecca. Through the poet he conveyed his message to the peoples wherever he travelled.

He died in 1539 and tradition records that, as the news spread that he was likely to die, Hindus and Muslims came for a last sight of the great man and there arose a dispute between them, the Hindu saying that he would cremate the Guru's body and the Muslim saying that he would bury it in accordance with Muslim custom. The dispute was eventually ended by the Guru himself. He told the Hindus to place flowers on his right and the Muslims to place flowers on his left, and whichever flowers were fresh on the following day, that side should dispose of his body according to their custom. Then the Guru covered his body with a sheet and he went to sleep. The following morning when the cover was removed both the right and the left flowers were fresh, but the body of Guru Nanak had gone!

This story, fact or fiction, points to the Guru's constant teaching – that there is no difference between a Hindu and a Muslim, then the main differing groups, and God was the same, whatever the method of worship.

The Sikhs continued in the steps of their first Guru for centuries, adding to the prayers and songs – hymns, really – until all these rules and praise and worship were gathered into one volume, and this has now become the scripture for all Sikhs – it is called the Guru Granth Sahib.

The golden age of Sikhism was under the reign of Maharajah Ranjit Singh. He employed both Hindu and Muslim in his armies which he organized on Western lines, with many Europeans among their officers, and for little over 40 years the Punjab became home, a real homeland, for the Sikhs.

At the time of Independence there were many Sikhs who hoped that the British Government would create a separate Sikh state in the Punjab, but this was not to be; yet still today there are hundreds of agitators among more militant Sikhs who continue to press for a separate State.

The Golden Temple at Amritsar as it now stands, encrusted with gold, approached by a causeway lined with golden railings and floored with marble, standing in the middle of the great tank of water known as the 'Pool of Immortality', is a lasting memorial to the great Ranjit Singh. In 1984 it made media headlines as the setting for Sikh unrest.

The Sikhs have a reputation for being volatile, war-like and hot-tempered; their first Guru was a Kshastria, one born into the fighting castes, so perhaps this is not to be wondered at. Most of the Sikh men seem to be incredibly tall and all but the most modern (referred to as 'mechanised' Sikhs) still wear the turban. Though this is not mandatory, there are some things that are and they are referred to as the five 'K's': the *kesh*, the *kangha*, the *kirpan*, the *kachs* and the *kara*. The *kesh* is the long uncut hair which distinguishes the Sikh and is the first rule to be obeyed contained in the Khalsa, the brotherhood of Sikhs. To keep this uncut hair tidy – and there is no one more fastidious than the Sikh – he uses a comb, or *kangha*. The *kirpan* is a sword that can be anything up to 90 cm (3 ft) in length. These days, because of various laws that forbid the carrying of offensive weapons, this frequently takes the form of a piece of metal embedded in the comb, or *kangha*. The *kachs* are short cotton trousers worn under long trousers, as underpants. When fighting, these short trousers were more practical than the dhoti, the loin cloth. The *kara* is a steel bracelet worn on the right wrist and, together with the turban, is the most noticeable symbol of a Sikh. In twentieth-century India, though, with fashion being all to the young, not everyone wearing a steel bracelet will be a Sikh, just as not all people with the surname Singh will be a Sikh; but all Sikhs have the name Singh! Singh means lion.

Sikhism could be described as the results of the efforts of a protestor against the old laws which, through preaching and example and disciple-ship, have led from a movement to a religion, with its scripture, its initiation rites, its rites of marriage and of death, and its places of pilgrimage.

The Sikhs practise tolerance and love for all (sometimes difficult to believe when one sees them in war-like mood pressing for the creation of a separate State), and in their Gurdwaras, their temples, they will welcome anyone and offer shelter and food to them and allow them to rest or stay for a while.

The Parsees

The Parsee religion (also spelt Parsi or Pharsi) is one of the oldest religions in the world, and believers are followers of the Prophet Zarathustra (Zoroastra) of the sixth century BC. Their God is Mazda, the God of Light.

III Travel

General information

Tourist Introduction Card; liquor permit; visas
On visiting India a Tourist Introduction Card can be very useful and is easily and freely available from any Tourist Office, usually somewhere at the point of entry into India. At the same time, a liquor permit can be obtained.

The Tourist Introduction Card will introduce the traveller to government authorities and departments from which he might wish assistance. The liquor permit is required in 'dry' States, such as Gujarat and Tamil Nadu. If you wish to drink, then it is better to do so legally. Needless to say, there is much disregard for the letter of the law.

For the visitor there is no shortage of good Indian spirits, but if imported liquor is desired, then the price will be high.

A visa may be necessary at the time of your entry into India so check with the authorities before leaving home. A three month visa actually only lasts for 90 days.

Income Tax Clearance Certificate
If your stay in India does not exceed 90 days you are free to leave without this. If your stay is 90 days or more, you will require this certificate which can be obtained from a local Income Tax office at the point of departure. Be advised, though; the process of obtaining one may take a whole day of battling with bureaucracy. If you are lucky, however, you could be in and out within half an hour.

It must be noted that neither a return half of an air ticket nor a new single or return ticket can be used or booked without this certificate in the case of a stay of more than 90 days.

Foreign travel tax
On departing from India there is a tax charged of 100 rupees per person, and travellers are well advised to keep this amount aside from other expenses so that on arrival at the airport the money is available. You will not be allowed to leave without paying and as departure times can be

disconcertingly late at night or early in the morning, facilities are not always open for changing traveller's cheques. The present foreign travel tax is high now, compared with not so long ago, when it was 20 rupees. For example, a family of four leaving India after a visit will have to pay the equivalent of £25 (1984). If multiplied by the thousands and thousands who depart from India each year it will be seen that there is revenue from this charge running into millions of rupees.

Health regulations

No special innoculations are needed on entering India if arriving from the United Kingdom. It is wise, though, to consult the Indian Tourist Department before leaving any country, making sure that enough time is allowed for any treatment, as there may be a change in regulations.

An injection of gamma globulin as a help towards avoiding infectious hepatitis is advisable. This is painless and produces no side-effects and will be given by your doctor. Should any outbreaks of cholera or smallpox occur whilst you are in India, it is a very simple thing to get innoculated on the spot. A valid certificate of vaccination against yellow fever is required of all persons entering India from an infected area; otherwise, a period of quarantine must be accepted. A list of infected areas is available from the Indian High Commission. The vaccine must have been approved by the World Health Organization and must have been administered at least ten days before arrival.

N.B. As Government Health Regulations frequently change, it is a good idea to check with your local health authority on innoculations which, as a safety measure, may be currently recommended.

Overland routes to India

Once so popular but, since the Soviet involvement in Afghanistan, now less so, the route from Europe to India has had to be modified. This makes it much more complicated and certainly less easy for the traveller to just get up and drive to India, as was previously possible.

The overland route most used now passes through France, Germany, Yugoslavia, Bulgaria, Turkey, Iran and thence to Pakistan. An alternative would be to travel by rail to Turkey and then by bus to Basra from where there are regular sailings to Bombay on cargo boats.

Going to India overland is still an adventure but not so much so as it was when the route was more clearly defined and less politically hazardous. The great thing is time; if you have enough time, then any route to India is possible.

Sea routes to India

The traditional sailing routes to India are no longer possible but some cargo ships are available and enquiries should be made in writing to such companies as British India Navigation Co., London, or Scindia Steamship

Co. in Bombay. The cost will be appropriate to the number of weeks you will be aboard, and the letting of accommodation is left to the ship's captain; but board and lodging, even on a cargo vessel, can be expensive.

Indian currency

Based on the rupee, it is divided into paises, of which there are 100 to a rupee. It is well to consider that an Indian will think in paises and not in rupees. Contrary to what the affluent will relate, there are very many everyday items in India that cost less than a rupee. For the tourist, though, for whom the currency is strange, it is simpler to think in rupees.

Indian Standard Time

Time in India is $5\frac{1}{2}$ hours ahead of G.M.T. and $4\frac{1}{2}$ hours ahead of Central European Time. It is $11\frac{1}{2}$ hours ahead of United States Time.

Travel in India

Around their own country the peoples of India are inveterate travellers. Rural and urban Indians will, at some time or another in their lives, travel a reasonable distance in India. It may be on a pilgrimage to a shrine or a temple or a mosque; or to attend a marriage ceremony or the anniversary of a friend's death, and it is very often to seek work.

It is mainly among the sophisticated Indians that travelling is undertaken for a holiday, and these travellers are particularly few. A holiday in the Western sense is not part of the Indian's life pattern. One of the results of this is the thousands of miles of virgin beach that trace India's coastline, most of which is seductively beautiful. So often though, it is too hot for comfort and too remote for development and the curving stretches of sand and palm are left to the fisher communities who are more interested in what comes out of the sea than in going in it themselves.

A beach holiday is a traditional holiday in the West but this is not so in India. Notwithstanding this there are beach resorts in India which cater

15 Hot sands on the Malabar Coast

for the Indians and for the Europeans. Goa has been encouraged by the government and has developed extensively as a tourist and conference centre and resort and has all the facilities that will make a Westerner feel 'at home', according to one brochure I read – the last thing a discerning traveller would wish! – and there are several other beach resorts.

Travel to and from townships and over the countryside is a constant activity. For the visitor, this near-excess of travelling facilities makes seeing the country quite easy, but a plan should be drawn up first and a resolve taken to stick to what has been decided.

For instance, it may be that you wish to tour around the temples of south India. If so, then the best time for visiting these places should be considered (see under the appropriate State) and the time spent in India be organized to agree with this. It would, for example, be more difficult to attempt such a tour during the monsoon season.

A tour of Moghul India, which is a popular group tour holiday package, would be disastrous if taken after April, as the weather would be so hot as to inhibit daytime travel, and problems would be a constant factor. Physical dehydration and torpor, breakdowns of services, the need for air-conditioning and exposure to intense heat would cause needless fatigue and possible illness.

Another time when tourist places become crowded beyond reason is during Indian festivals, and to go on what is an expensive tour when one simply cannot move around is another hazard to be avoided. This applies as much to the group tourist, who is restricted to a set schedule, as to the lone traveller making his own arrangements. If there is enough time in hand, then any itinerary throughout India is possible. As with most travel, the more leisurely manner in which one proceeds, the fuller the experience.

For the people who have to cram as many as possible of the sights of India into a short time, the only feasible way would be by pre-booked air travel. If more time is available, then sleeper compartments on trains are a useful way of keeping days free for sight-seeing, using some if not all nights for travel

Bus travel is slower and much more leisurely and one can travel amazing distances and see more of the country on or from the train. Luxury buses are comfortable and speedy, but you may have to watch a long film via video in a language that you do not understand.

Any arrangements made in advance may have to be paid for in sterling or dollars before arriving in India.

An Indian might say that the only way to see his country, travelling at the correct pace, is by bullock cart, but few people these days would have the time for such indulgence – except, perhaps, Indians themselves!

The railway system

The Indian railway system is the second largest railway in the world and the largest in Asia.

The present system is an amalgamation of eight Pioneer Companies (listed at the end of this chapter) and the first railway route was opened in India in April, 1853, and ran from Bombay to Thana, a distance of 34 km (21 miles). This train consisted of 14 teak carriages and carried 400 passengers. By 1870 there were 7680 km (4772 miles) of track connecting the Gangetic Plain and the Central Provinces with Pune (Poona) and Madras, in the south.

With the opening of the Suez Canal in 1869, India became closer to Europe, the consequence being a frenzy of activity, with the railway system opening yet more miles of track so that by 1871 there was a direct line from Bombay to Calcutta and from Bombay to Madras.

Development afterwards progressed rapidly until at the turn of the century there was a total of 39,834 km (24,752 miles) of track. By 1947, the year of Independence, this total had swollen to a formidable 65,217 km (40,524 miles). Although at Independence and with the separation of India from Pakistan, India 'lost' 10,523 km (6539 miles) of track to the new Muslim country, she was still left with 54,693 km (33,985 miles) and an ever-increasing industry so that by now there are again over 64,374 km (40,000 miles) of rail track.

In 1948 there were 42 different railway systems of which 32 were owned by the Indian States. The Nizam of Hyderabad, for instance, controlled 2,246 km (1,396 miles) of rail track.

These State railways were nationalized by the Indian Government in April 1950 and the whole railway system was reshaped into six zones, later to be altered, until on 31st March, 1972, the entire railway system was government controlled with the exception of 644 km (400 miles) of narrow gauge.

The increase of tourist traffic is very much a part of Indian Railway's planning and it must be remembered that this means Indians travelling in India, which they do by the million, daily, as well as foreign tourists.

Concessional fares are available on most routes, such as the hill station journeys, with circular tour tickets for a good period, the exact time being chosen by the traveller. It may be for seven days or for 90 days. It should be noted that an Indrail pass does *not* guarantee a seat, whatever the class, on any train. Reservations and bookings should be made in the ordinary way, using the Indrail pass only to fulfil the requirements for cheaper travel.

Since 1964, the Taj Express has taken thousands of tourists to and from Delhi to Agra, the attraction being the Taj Mahal. One can leave New Delhi in the morning and be back the same night. The train is met by luxury buses, seats for which are bookable in advance. For the enthusiast's information, the train is pulled by W.P.-type bullet-nosed engines in blue and white livery which were built some time between 1947 and 1967.

Undoubtedly, the small-gauge routes are the most fascinating in India. The rack railway running from the small town of Mettupalayam to Coonoor, en route for Ootacamund in the Nilgiri Hills in south India, is one example. Small Swiss engines push blue and white coaches up incredible gradients through magnificent scenery. When the gradient becomes too steep, a catch mechanism underneath the engine lowers and engages the rack-rail.

The most famous mountain railway in India is the up and down to Darjeeling from Siliguri, which has been operating since 1880. The oldest engine, 'The Mountaineer', was built in 1892. It is time-consuming to go to Darjeeling and use this toy-train both ways, but you can fly direct to Darjeeling and then take the train back; you will certainly never forget the experience.

Over recent years many innovations have been introduced on the Indian railway system. Aircraft-type seating in air-conditioned comfort, yet at a fraction of the cost of first class fares, is but one of them.

There is, too, the now famous 'Palace on Wheels'. This train consists of carriages once used by the Maharajahs and designed especially for them. The coaches bear the ornate coats of arms, such as Jaipur, Mewar, Bhavnagar and, the oldest one, that of the Maharajah of Bikaner. This coach was built in 1898, and it was in such comfort that the Maharajahs and their retinues crossed India. In all, there are 13 carriages dating from 1890–1930, which run on a metre-gauge track. There are two restaurant cars and a lounge-observation car and, needless to say, servants galore. The train travels across Rajasthan visiting Jaipur, Udaipur, Jaisalmer, Jodhpur, Bharatpur and Agra and leaves from and returns to New Delhi. At over £1000 a trip, for eleven nights, it is expensive; but it is unique.

There are many famous trains that cross India and they have romantic and attractive names. The Coromandel Express, for instance, which runs from Calcutta to Madras; the Frontier from Bombay to New Delhi; the Gitanjili Express from Calcutta to Bombay; the Grand Trunk Express from Madras to New Delhi; the Brindavan Express from Madras to Bangalore; the Ganga Kaveri Express from Madras to Rameswaram; and a recently introduced one called the Udayan Express taking one from Bombay to Bangalore without changing – a great relief, as the change was always in the middle of the night.

Sleeping accommodation on Indian trains must always be reserved in advance and a reservation ticket extra to a journey ticket obtained. On arrival at the station your name will be found posted on a passenger list, much like the old passenger ships' lists and one should check both the number of the bogey (carriage) and the compartment number in that bogey and then proceed accordingly; the porters (called coolies) who will be carrying your bags will know the correct place on the platform at which to wait if the train is not in the station, and if it is waiting he will know where to take you.

The actual sleeping arrangements can be either a coupé (a compartment for two) or a compartment for four. The coupé is usually given to a married couple, but if a strong enough request is made for one, it can be arranged. Some of the older rolling-stock still has the coupé with the attached bathroom, otherwise all recent bogeys have this facility at each end. One of them will be with Eastern plumbing (i.e. the squat-type lavatory) and the other will be the conventional Western type. There will be a shower in the roof, not always immediately seen, but it is there and will be painted in 'railway green', a pale grey-green that spreads throughout all Indian trains from the corridors to the rexine seating. Beware of the shower, though, for if used during the daytime the water may scald you, being solar-heated, with the water tanks on the roof of the train!

If bedding is needed, then it can be obtained by reserving it in advance and obtaining another ticket. Bedding is called a 'bed roll', which it literally is – a rolled up collection of pillow, pillow-case, sheet, blanket and towel, all scrupulously clean. The bogey attendant will bring it to you and, when the time comes for sleep, make it up for you; in the morning he will come again and check each item and take it away. The charge for this is five rupees.

Porterage is always available at stations and airports and bus stands. At the railway stations the coolies wear red shirts and coats and a red turban which they wind around their heads as a sweat band. They will have, or should have, an arm band on their upper arm on which is written their registered number.

The charge used to be one rupee a bag or piece of luggage, no matter what the distance carried. The coolies, though, have not been slow to understand today's inflation and they see Westerners, or indeed any foreigner, as fair game from which to demand exorbitant money. At two rupees a bag, even these days, a coolie will be doing quite well and will be receiving more than an Indian would pay him. If, therefore, a traveller sticks at two rupees per item of luggage, the coolie will see that he is being fairly treated and will cease to argue.

In Indian economics there is a rate for most jobs, and foreign travellers, either in innocence or ignorance, upset this by giving rupees away too generously because to them it seems very little money. To an Indian, though, one rupee is a hundred paises. The sensible way to travel in any country is by observing the economics that prevail and trying to stick to them.

India is no exception in that many of the trains run late but I think a special case can be made for this enormous railway network. The last time I travelled from Bombay to Calcutta the train was 15 minutes late but the distance travelled was over 2000 km (1200 miles).

Rail travel is a marvellous way of seeing India and the comfort of a first class non-air-conditioned booking, though not decoratively attractive in the Western sense, is nevertheless adequate. Meals can be had as well as non-alcoholic drinks and fruit, and there is also a small library of paperbacks on some trains.

To travel first class air-conditioned is really to travel in style, but it doubles the cost and, for the money, many would rather fly.

A recent addition to rail travel is the introduction of the 'Hotel on Wheels' train. The Department of Tourism, in collaboration with the Railway Ministry, has launched the 'Hotel on Wheels' as a de-luxe train, completely air-conditioned, with a vestibule and lounge, bar, de-luxe sleeperettes and . . . a prayer room! The aim of the train is to provide all the luxury of a five-star hotel. It starts from Calcutta and takes tourists to Bodh Gaya, Gaya, Varanasi (Benares), Gorakhpur and back to Calcutta, including excursions to such places as Nalanda, Rajgir, Bodhgaya, Sarnath, Lumbini and Kushinagar.

The following eight companies, when amalgamated, formed The Old Guaranteed Railway Company which, since Independence, has become Indian Railways:

The East India Railway Company (1849)
The Great Indian Peninsular Railway Company (1844)
The Madras Guaranteed Railway Company (1852)
The Bombay, Baroda and Central India Railway Company (1855)
The Sind and Punjab and Delhi Railway Company (1856)
The Eastern Bengal Railway Company (1858)
The Great Southern Railway Company of India (1858)
The Calcutta and South Eastern Railway Company (1859)

George Stephenson, of 'The Rocket' fame, was one of the Directors of The Great Indian Peninsular Railway Company.

For railway buffs, the Delhi Railway Museum is well worth a visit. It is situated quite a way from, say, Connaught Circus, and is a good taxi ride to Chanakyapuri. Leave a whole morning for the visit.

Air travel

Indian Airlines operates all the internal air routes of India except those of Air India, which continue across the sub-continent from the main places of entry.

Unlike the glossy-brochure presentation and the slick advertising, which lead one to expect a service of comfort and efficiency, Indian Airlines only partly lives up to its projected image.

Planes are late, passengers too many for the service, booking systems are corrupt and, unaccountably, the air hostesses, usually international angels of the air, can be plain unhelpful. Many of the cabin staff consider lavatory duty, sickness care and floor cleanliness not to be part of their responsibility. Baggage reclamation often takes longer than the flight and some smaller airports are lamentably short of even basic facilities.

Forewarned is forearmed and so the generous traveller should make allowances – a noble generosity these days, as the cost of air travel in India has become so expensive.

Indian Airlines does handle a massive amount of traffic and this is mostly Indian. Booking seats is a highly competitive business and agents are accustomed to all sorts of dodges to ensure a reservation – double booking, for instance, and then cancelling one ticket, in order to make sure of a place on the plane. Some seats are 'reserved' for government 'servants' who may or may not turn up for departure.

The whole process of air travel in India is, or so it appears to many, a glorified muddle. But if you make sure that your bookings are made through a reputable agent, that they are correct and are *confirmed* 24 hours before departure, then you should at least get on the plane!

Only ten years ago things were different. Then, travel by air within India was less frenetic, was more predictably guaranteed, was a welcoming experience with smaller planes and friendly crews; it might be said that there was a pioneering spirit present. This was before expansion and the arrival of larger planes which meant more people to handle, though with the same ground facilities. Now the system only works in parts and therefore schedules get behind and passengers get frustrated and airports crowded. In the monsoon season this can be so wearing that the alternative of train travel seems luxuriously accommodating.

According to the map, and all things being as they should, the cities of India are well connected by air and, with much advance planning and a good agent, there should be no problems other than those met with in any country.

There is a 'Discover India' ticket which permits unlimited travel on domestic routes at a concessional price. Seeing India this way can be a great rush round, keeping to flight schedules which, if not on time, could jeopardize a whole arranged tour. One has to take the optimistic view and believe that this will not be so, otherwise this concession would be useless; but it is wise to remember that it only needs one plane to be late to upset plans, and if your time is short or is controlled in any way, then it is better to be more flexible than the 'Discover India' ticket would allow.

You must, incidentally, pay for air tickets either in foreign currency or with rupees for which you can show a bank encashment certificate.

Travel by road

The bus and coach services in India have improved by leaps and bounds in recent years and most important centres are now connected by a luxury bus service.

Each State has its own ordinary bus service which runs from the capital city to outlying districts. This form of travel can be very arduous, and you really need to be dogged and/or passionately gregarious to squash into these uncomfortable buses along with a hundred others in a bus built for 40! The accident rate for these buses is quite high so an added qualification for travelling in them, other than masochism, would be bravery.

An alternative is the luxury bus or coach. The cost of this form of transport is amazingly low and the standard of comfort relatively high. Most have aircraft-type seating which reclines and makes night travel very popular. Again, it must be stressed that booking ahead on most routes is essential, though in the case of buses two or three days would be sufficient.

Coach tours are also numerous, especially at tourist centres such as Calcutta, Bangalore, New Delhi, Mysore and Jaipur, but be cautioned – *video has come to India* and companies who run coaches have not been slow to install it, loud and strident, in both local tours and in long-distance journeys. Indians, in the majority, love it. They find it quite fascinating. The bus companies seem to believe that their customers are deaf and so they turn up the volume as loud as possible and there is absolutely no escape. Ear-plugs are, therefore, advisable.

The film shown will be in the local language and will last at least two hours; it does not matter how bright the sunshine is outside the coach, the show will go on, as the coaches are fitted with smoked glass windows and thick curtains behind which, regardless of the scenery outside, the Indian travellers sit glued to the screen in absolute bliss, being deafened, and loving it!

A reasonable compromise would be to fit the type of listening ear-pieces that are found on aircraft, but I have not found one that has this facility. Video coaches are now big business and if one wishes to travel this way, then one has to accept the trend.

There was a cartoon in an Indian newspaper showing a bus terminus where a wife was talking to her husband about a passenger who had left the queue. She was saying, 'Instead of going to Bangalore, he is going to Kanpur. He says that that bus is showing a film he has not seen.' It was an apt comment on the video craze that has swept the whole of India.

Car hire on a self-drive basis is not available in India but one can rent a car with a driver, and, although expensive, this is the best thing to do. The driver will speak the local language and will also mend any punctures, something that regularly happens in India due to the road surfaces.

Shared taxis are a common alternative to both buses and car hire. You will probably have to wait until the driver has at least five other passengers, but the journey will be more intimate and more fun than the bus and will certainly work out less expensive than a hire car.

Hill stations

Through literature and through endless anecdotes by the British Raj residents, hill stations have had woven around them a folk-lore that belongs nowhere else, unless it be Cheltenham-cum-Grasmere. The past glory of well laid out lawns leading to pedimented Regency club buildings, of bungalows built amongst the trees or around a lake, with their 'English' gardens, their pretty gables and 'homesy' names has gradually faded. The kept-up look has almost disappeared and decay is setting in apace. This would be denied with vehemence and passion by the few Britishers who still remain in the hills. It is a case of familiarity dimming the eye. To a visitor, though, fresh from the well-kept aspect of either a Cheltenham or a Grasmere, the crumbling graveyard, the lifeless club, the overgrown gardens that front bungalows crying out for a lick of paint, could be a disappointment. For those who once lived up in the hills and had made such a gracious life there (albeit alien to the country in which they were living) to revisit these havens of retreat from the heat would be, to say the least, a shock.

This same decrepitude has overtaken the old Cantonment areas of towns and cities throughout India. They have become overpopulated and undermaintained, so that they now wear a very forlorn look.

It is wise, therefore, to remember that India is for the Indians now and, whilst some of the old customs of hill station life are continued, others have died beneath the new identity that Indians have given to these places. Summer palaces of Maharajahs have become institutes or colleges; clubs have largely ceased their social functions; only a few bungalows are properly maintained; light industry has infiltrated the hills and, with it, more people have made an assortment of homes there. Hotels have sprung up to cater for the Indian traveller and businessman.

One can still have a 'gracious experience' staying at a hill station but it will not be one where every aspect pleases. Some things will be incongruous and, rather than to try and pick out these differences, it is far better to enjoy what are now Indian hill stations, with their fantastic views from high points, and numerous pathways and glades, and to be spoilt by the very caring and comfortable better-class hotels where standards and customs are kept up.

Many tours include a visit to a hill station on their itinerary but, when booking, be warned that these places out of *their* particular season can be chilly, if not very cold. Many tours leave for India throughout December and January in order to be there when the weather is most pleasant, but any hill station then would be on a par with the Scottish Highlands, to which they are so often, topographically, compared. From February onwards to the peak season of May, June and early July they are fine and warm, often hot during the daytime and, by June, warm during the night also. It is at this time that the flower shows and horse trials are held, and also some hunting, but few tours venture forth to India during May, June and July!

Mussoorie
Less visited than most hill stations, this one, referred to as 'The Gay Perch in The Hills' in old guide-books, still does keep up many of the old ways. The Mall, for instance, is still prohibited to motor cars, and here one can have tea and gaze out over the plains 2133 m (7,000 ft) below.

Simla
Not often seen on tour itineraries, Simla was one of the most important British hill stations in northern India; it became the hot weather seat of

government during the time of the British and a favourite place for taking leave and for sending families to in order to escape the heat of the plains. Here, too, there is a Mall and the British banned not only all vehicles but, until the 1914–18 war, all Indians. Nowadays it is a holiday place for Indians and independent foreign travellers, and has many relics of the Raj, from Viceregal Lodge downwards.

Ootacamund

This is the 'queen of hill stations', which now has a rather tarnished crown, yet all it needs is a good polish. This may seem a rather glib or facile comment but when a place has such a high reputation as Ootacamund, such thoughts can be provoked in the mind of a visitor who, on getting there, sees the lack of care for the place that is all around. Not within the purlieus of the fine hotels (and one can be very comfortable indeed at Ootacamund) but all around, when out and about, it is disappointingly seedy. One is led to expect so much. It is, though, not impossible to put on rose-tinted glasses and view Ootacamund uncritically. After all, one goes there to enjoy oneself and there are plenty of the usual diversions of hill stations, walks and view-points, horse riding and botanical gardens (these are really beautiful) and high peaks up which to clamber. The journey to Ootacamund, though, is an experience really to be enjoyed, whether by bus, through the rain forests and tea gardens or eucalyptus groves up winding roads past villages, or via the toy-train, The Nilgiri Mountain Railway, from Coimbatore to Mettupalayam and then on by bus via Coonoor to Ootacamund; it is well worth the effort.

Try to arrange not to leave Ooty (as Ootacamund is more often called) by the way you arrived but via bus or car (shared taxi) to Mysore or Bangalore. This way you will go down the other side of the Nilgiri Hills and through the Mudumalai Wildlife Sanctuary. A visit to the Sanctuary can also be made as an excursion from Ooty. The bus takes little over two hours and it is a glorious ride to Theppukadu village where there is the reception centre for the sanctuary and from where visits can be made into the interior of the forest. There will not be much wild life to see from the road but there is every chance that a herd of elephants will cross in front of the bus.

Kodaikanal

A quieter place than Ootacamund, Kodaikanal is really one of the most beautiful places in south India. To reach it one has to go up from the eastern side of the hills, from Madurai Road township. Here there will be a bus, or one can take a taxi (alone or shared). The climate is more equable on the eastern side of the Nilgiris, and Kodaikanal has a more or less even temperature apart from the chill months of December, January and February. It is most attractive in the late season of September and October but has the usual hill station season of April, May and June. After

June, the rains start and will continue until around mid-September. There is a 5 km (3 mile) long promenade around the lake, and boats can be hired.

Mount Abu

Another accessible hill station and one that is quite different from any other, here the terrain is open and rocky and covered in palm trees and volcanic mounds. Many pilgrims come here to see the Dilwara Temple of the Jains, described as the most wondrous marble carving anywhere in the world. For anyone interested in architecture, the Dilwara Temples at Mount Abu are enough justification for visiting this out-of-the-way place. It is actually in Rajasthan, just on the southern tip which leads into Gujarat. One has to entrain for Mount Abu by going to Abu Road township and then taking a bus or car to the top. All trains are met by transport, even those which arrive in the middle of the night.

Matheran

Like many hill stations, there is a toy-train, or narrow gauge train, up to Matheran. This is the nearest hill station to Bombay and is a contrast to bustling city life. It is an excursion worth making if time is on hand when staying in Bombay. One goes via Neral, which is on the Bombay-Pune (Poona) railway line. The narrow gauge train winds and twists through fields and woods for 20 km (12 miles) and the rise is a sheer delight. Unless one were an avid and determined walker one would not want to stay up at Matheran for very long, but long enough to see the spectacular sunsets and to gaze for miles westwards to where, in the distance, one can see the Arabian Sea. There is no prohibition at Matheran about motor vehicles because there are none! From Neral there is nothing but a rickshaw for transport, or shank's pony. Of all the hill stations, Matheran is perhaps the prettiest and the most unspoilt. On the way up, small boys will leap on and off the train selling drinks and *jambul*, a dark red fruit. Drink the drink, as long as you can buy a sealed bottle, but beware of the fruit – it needs washing before eating and even then may cause acidity.

Mahabaleshwar

Another Maharashtran hill station and not too far from Bombay, Mahabaleshwar is near to Pune (Poona). It is popular with both those from Pune and Bombay and, during the season, will be full of families escaping for a time the pre-monsoon heat. One reaches Mahabaleshwar via Pune from where there are luxury buses or taxis by which to go the final 120 km (74 miles). Before reaching Mahabaleshwar one reaches Panchgani, meaning 'five hills', also a hill station but smaller and without all the facilities of Mahabaleshwar. Really, though, for the foreign visitor each place is interchangeable and both can be made the point of what can be a long and tedious journey. It will take the better part of two days to get there from Bombay. At Mahabaleshwar there are places like Elphinstone Point, Arthur's Seat (memories of Edinburgh, but what a different view!) and Chinaman's Waterfall. Long walks through enchanting woodlands and views are the chief attraction at this highest of the hill stations in western India (1371 m [4500 ft]) which was once the summer seat of the government of the Bombay Presidency.

Darjeeling

Darjeeling gets its name from two Tibetan words 'Dorje Ling', which mean 'Place of the Thunderbolt'. Legend tells of Sonan Gragpa, a dignitary during the time of the fifth Dalai Lama, who was a very learned man. Because of his popularity, rival priests were jealous of him and attempted to kill him, but he escaped. Eventually he renounced the world and committed suicide and it is said that the smoke from his funeral pyre assumed the form of a thunderbolt, threatening to destroy his enemies. After placating his angry spirit he was adopted as a protective deity in the Buddhist pantheon under the name 'Mighty Thunderbolt'.

Originally a lamasery stood on the hill now called Darjeeling. Sikkim ceded the village of Darjeeling to the British in 1835 who themselves, attracted to its cool climate and beautiful scenery, made it into the hill station now so popular. One wonders if it would have become so internationally known had not a type of tea been named after it, but Darjeeling tea is a speciality all over the world. Darjeeling is 669 km (416 miles) from Calcutta by rail to Siliguri – an overnight journey where one changes to the narrow gauge mountain railway and puffs up the last 80 km (50 miles) in one of the most thrilling toy-train journeys in the world. One can go by air from Calcutta.

Festivals and fairs

A festival in India will, more often than not, be connected in some way with a faith. India has seen the birth of three of the important religions of the world – Hinduism, Buddhism and Jainism; and many others have become established in the country and have flourished in India's unique climate of religious tolerance. Two such are Islam and Christianity. The majority of people in India are, though, Hindus and it is from this philosophy that sprang Buddhism, Jainism and, much later on, Sikhism.

India has the second largest Muslim population in the world, a population from which have emerged many great men, such as Akbar, the Mughal Emperor, for instance, who sponsored Persian translations of the great Hindu epics, the Ramayana and the Mahabharata.

Christianity came to India earlier than almost everywhere else outside the Middle East. Saint Thomas is believed to have come to south India in the first century. The Syrian Christian Church of south India, predominant in Kerala, traces its roots to conversions by Saint Thomas. Marco Polo, who visited Kerala in 1293, refers to the 'Nestorian' Christians he met there. In 1544 St Francis Xavier spent three months in Kerala and

16 Old photo of Darjeeling town – the Himalayas in the background

built the Chapel of Kottar. Today there are 11 million Christians in India.

The Parsees, followers of Zoroastra, came to India from Persia during the eighth century, seeking shelter from religious persecution. They are now an important and prosperous community, living mainly in Gujarat and Maharashtra.

Throughout India all religions enjoy full equality and the followers of each faith celebrate their feasts in a bewildering number of annual festivals. Many of the Hindu holidays are linked with harvest, and seemingly every change of season is celebrated in song and dance. Other holidays honour mythological deities or are entirely religious, involving fasting and special prayers.

It is not likely, therefore, that a visitor to India will miss being able to join in a festival; he only needs to be in the right place at the right time!

There follows a list of festivals arranged from January to December, and the places where it is most likely that they can be enjoyed; also, only approximate dates are given, as so many depend on the moon.

January

Pongal, or Sankranti   Celebrated throughout Tamil Nadu, Andhra Pradesh and Karnataka and especially in Tiruchiripalli (Trichinopoly) and Madurai: a three-day festival and one of the biggest in these areas of south India. On the first day the sun is worshipped and all houses are cleaned. On the next day cows and bullocks are a part of thanksgiving ceremonies and are fed on specially cooked rice. The beasts are decorated with flowers and paint and in the evening are led around village and town in procession to the beat of crude drums and flute music. On the third day in some towns in the south there are bull-fights in which young men try to wrest bundles of currency notes from the horns of ferocious bulls. The bulls are not killed for they will have to return to their life of toil and, often, torture, after their one day of release from plough or cart.

Republic Day This national festival of India is observed throughout the country to mark the inauguration of the Republic of India on 26 January 1950. In Delhi, the celebrations include a magnificent parade of the armed forces and of civilians from all the States. The parade ends with a fly-past of zooming jets and 'dancing' helicopters. The President of India takes the salute whilst in the States, where there are also separate parades, the Governor of the State takes the salute. If you are in New Delhi at this time, then try and make sure of a seat on one of the stands that line the route. This is one procession in which you will see bedecked and bejewelled elephants, and the famous Camel Corps. In the evening there will be colourful folk-dance programmes.

Shivratri Celebrated by Hindus all over India, Shivratri is a festival devoted to the worship of Lord Shiva. Devotees spend the night singing songs in his praise. Special celebrations are held at important temples such as those at Chidambaram, Varanasi (Benares), Kalahasti, Srisailam and Kharjuraho.

Bakr-Id, or Id-ul-Zuha Chief centres are New Delhi, Lucknow, Calcutta and Hyderabad, where Muslims observe this festival to commemorate the Prophet Ibrahim (Abraham) offering his son for sacrifice. Rams and goats are sacrificed, new clothes are worn and there is feasting and rejoicing.

February

Muharram This commemorates the martyrdom of Iman Hussain, the grandson of the Prophet Mohammed. Tazias (see section on Islam), which are symbolic of the martyr's tomb at Karbala, are carried in mourning processions. The most famous Muharram procession is to be seen at Lucknow.

March

Holi The most boisterous of India's festivals, it is observed all over northern India. Men, women and children throw coloured water and powder over one another. Sweetmeats are exchanged between friends. If you don't mind being squirted with colour, then brave the streets – and brave is an appropriate word. Any European would be a special target and enthusiasm often overcomes commonsense. The crowds are dense and items quite different from coloured water are often thrown by the vulgar. European women should not go out into the streets. Visitors may celebrate Holi in a delightful way within the confines of their hotel or, if staying with a family, as advised by them. In Rajasthan, at Jaipur, the Holi Elephant Festival is now held. A procession makes its way through the streets to the Changan Stadium, and it is a majestic procession indeed,

17 Typical temple car festival

made up of elephants, caparisoned and bedecked with jewels and painted howdahs. To see this event is to witness a little of India's fabulous and indulgent past. Besides the elephants there are polo matches, races, dancing and song contests. It is a very gay time, strikingly colourful, radiant and dazzling, and if the beautiful city of Jaipur could be enhanced, then at Holi it is.

May

Buddha Purnima   Celebrating the birth, enlightenment, death and salvation of the Lord Buddha, this is especially relevant in the State of Bihar.

June/July

Car Festival   This is the time when temple cars, huge wooden structures on wheels which carry the God, make their processions. The most famous and spectacular is at Puri, in Orissa, when over a million people cram the route to see Lord Jagannath being pulled in the enormous temple chariot by teams of men. Once, devotees would throw themselves under the wheels of the chariots and kill themselves, thus attaining Nirvanah. This suicide is now banned.

August

Independence Day – 15 August   This is the anniversary of India's independence from Britain in 1947. There are no special celebrations but the Prime Minister makes a speech from the ramparts of the Red Fort at Delhi. The event is, of course, televised to the nation.

Onam   The greatest festival in the State of Kerala, Onam is primarily a harvest festival. It is observed in every home and in open public places.

18 Boats taking part in the Snake Boat Race

One of the main events is the Snake Boat Races held at several places along the palm-fringed lagoons of Kerala. The boats are long and sleek and have variously carved 'heads'; some are beak-shaped, like a bird, others are kite-tailed or resemble a lion or dragon. Competition is fierce and suitable places from which to watch this colourful spectacle should be reserved, begged or bagged long before dawn, either at Kottayam or Aranmula.

Janmasthami   The birth anniversary of Lord Krishna, believed to be the reincarnation of Vishnu and author of the Bhagavadgita, this is celebrated all over India but especially at Mathura and Brindavan (Mysore), places where Lord Krishna spent his childhood. In Bombay, Delhi and Agra special performances are enacted, often by children, of scenes from Lord Krishna's early life.

October

Gandhi Jayanti   The anniversary of the birth of Mahatma Gandhi, celebrated throughout the land. At the Rajghat, Delhi, where Gandhi's body was cremated, there is a special ceremony with prayers.

Dussera, or Durga Puja   This is a ten-day festival based on the epic, Ramayana, signifying the triumph of good over evil. It is perhaps the most popular festival in India. Every region observes the festival in some way. In northern India it is known as Ram Lila and there are plays and presentations of dance and music recalling the doings of the legendary hero of the Ramayana, Rama. On the tenth day processions collect at public grounds, there to burn the often enormous effigies of Ravana, which will be stuffed with fireworks and which will explode before thousands of spectators. It is in West Bengal that this festival is known as

Durga Puja, since the Goddess Durga aided Rama in his defeat of Ravana. Ahmedabad and Mysore and Baroda are other centres of interest, Baroda being especially alive with the graceful Garba dancing in the streets. It is great fun to be around during this time, really anywhere, but especially in either West Bengal or Gujarat. The food, too, will be special and marvellous.

November

Diwali This is an occasion for great rejoicing and excitement and perhaps the happiest of Indian festivals, when innumerable lamps are lit in niches and windows and on pavements and in trees and floated on lakes and down streams and rivers. The lights are symbolic of lamps lit to show Rama his way home from his many adventures. This festival is also dedicated to the Goddess Lakshmi, particularly in Bombay and in the State of Gujarat. Here it will be very noisy for at least ten days. The people let off fireworks and bombs – really loud bangers. Businessmen vie with each other to set off the loudest and most continuous series of bangs. It is a propitious way of saluting the Goddess Lakshmi, who happens to be the Goddess of wealth!

In Bengal they worship the Goddess Kali, she who symbolizes strength. Spectacular images of Kali are made and worshipped and then, seemingly like all images in Indian festivals (with the exception of Ravana), they are immersed in a river or in some convenient water.

Coming on the top of Dussera and its festivities, this is an interesting time to be in India.

Id-ul-Fitr, Ramadan This Muslim festival marks the end of Ramadan, the Muslim month of fasting, and is an occasion for feasting and

19 Delhi – Parliament building lit at Diwali festival

rejoicing. The mosques are full and so are homes, being visited by friends and relatives exchanging good wishes and greetings. The festival is a moveable one, varying in date from year to year.

December

Feast of St Xavier Celebrated on 3 December, this is one of the most important festivals in Goa. It marks the mission of St Xavier in India, special masses are said in the churches and there are processions. Other parts of India where this feast is celebrated are Bangalore, Daman, Bombay and the State of Kerala.

Christmas time Christmas is observed in much splendour throughout the churches in India with carol singing and, especially in Goa and Daman and the south, by colourful processions. Pageants are staged telling the story of Christmas, but, unlike in the West, the sun will be shining, brightly lighting the festivities, and the air will be warm, and it is an unusual experience for travellers from cold countries.

In Bombay a Pontifical High Mass is held in the open air at the Cooperage Gardens. In New Delhi services are held at the Sacred Heart Church and St Paul's Cathedral. In Tamil Nadu Christmas is a time for dance festivals and evenings of classical Carnatic music.

Christmas Day is a declared public holiday all over India.

Fairs

As distinct from festivals, fairs have very much a business air, not being governed by any religious event. They are a periodical gathering for the sale of goods, often with entertainment, exhibitions and quite a lot of chicanery.

The most colourful of fairs is at Pushkar, 11 km (7 miles) from Ajmer in Rajasthan. The fair is noted for the sale of camels. Races are held in which riders on gaily decorated camels show off the speed and manoeuvrability of their mounts. On the final day of the Pushkar Fair, prizes are awarded and a kind of musical chairs is played by the camel riders. It is one of the most fascinating sights and not to be missed if one is in the area. Many tours take in this event. November is the time, but it can be cold, especially at night, so warm clothing is advised.

There are two other fairs worth noting. One is similar to the Pushkar Fair but is intended for the sale of cattle, not camels, and takes place at Sonepur, a small township situated on the banks of the Ganges near Patna in the State of Bihar in north-east India. This fair is much more basic but none the less interesting, though perhaps more to the specialist in culture and customs than to the tourist.

The other fair is a movable one and depends on a solar eclipse. Indeed, it takes place only at the time of an eclipse and is mainly celebrated in the north in centres like Allahabad, Hardwar, Varanasi (Benares) and

20 Thronging pilgrims at Benares; priests sit beneath rattan umbrellas dispensing prayers

especially at Kurukshetra, in Haryana State. A solar eclipse is an occasion when pious Hindus bathe in rivers and pay homage to their ancestors.

Thousands of pilgrims congregate at rivers all over India, especially along the length of the Ganges. The biggest crowd, though, is at Kurukshetra, the site of the legendary battlefield of the Mahabharata. It was here that Lord Krishna explained the philosophy of the Bhagavad-gita.

It is amazing that so many people will immerse themselves joyously in the chill waters when the air, too, is cold in a place like Hardwar. Here the waters of the Ganges, fresh from the melting snows of the Himalayas, are freezing even in summertime.

Some game sanctuaries

Jungles, rivers and lakes all over India provide a fine habitat for wild life: animals such as the tiger, the national animal of India, for instance, and the one-horned rhinoceros, the snow leopard, the wild ass and the Asiatic lion. The latter is found only at one sanctuary, in Gujarat.

Wild life sanctuaries have been established all over India in order to preserve and protect the fauna, and at the same time they also protect flowers and trees.

For the nature lover they offer a unique opportunity to see animals and birds in natural settings. Shooting is forbidden other than for natural environmental control purposes.

The Gir Forest (Gujarat)
Situated in south Gujarat, one can fly there from Bombay or can visit the reserve from Junagadh or from Ahmedabad. The best season is from October to May. Gir is the home of the Indian lion; in fact, it is the only place outside zoos where lions can be seen.

Corbett National Park (Uttar Pradesh)
Named after the famous hunter and author, Jim Corbett, the park is situated in the foothills of the Himalayas on the banks of the Ram Ganga river, where crocodiles lurk. The park is the haunt of tiger, leopard, deer and wild elephant. The best time for visiting is between December and May.

Mudumalai and Bandipur (Tamil Nadu/Karnataka)
Situated on the borders of Tamil Nadu and Karnataka, this sanctuary is divided by a river from which many animals and birds can be seen. Herds of gaur (the Indian bison) and spotted deer are common, as also are elephants.

Jeeps, trucks and riding elephants are available for safari and there are excellent motor roads linking observation points and viewing towers. A bus I was once travelling on here was nearly charged over by a leading elephant of a wild herd, a rare sight as these animals are quite used to humans and their transport.

This sanctuary is easy of access from Mysore or Bangalore, or from Ootacamund during November to March.

Kanha Kisli (Madhya Pradesh)
In the heart of Madhya Pradesh and known for tiger, this has rest houses and riding elephants and jeep transport. It is near Nagpur, Jabalpur and Raipur. There is a good hotel, the Mayura, at Raipur, from where this reserve is about six hours by road. The reserve is extensive and extremely beautiful and well worth a detour. You would need two days there. November to March are good times.

Nagarhole (Karnataka)
At a distance of 200 km (125 miles) from Bangalore and 65 km (40 miles) from Mysore, Nagarhole gets its name from the snake, for which the local name is Naga. The name means 'Serpentine River'. It is a small paradise of a reserve, 18 km (11 miles) in extent and fine for picnics. There is an assortment of wild life to be seen and many beautiful birds. The best time for visiting is from October to May, preferably in the early mornings.

Kaziranga (Assam)

This is the home of the one-horned Asian rhinoceros, which only wild life protection has saved from extinction; other animals to be seen here are wild buffalo, sambar, swamp deer and wild elephant. The best season to visit is from February to May.

Bandhavgarh (Madhya Pradesh)

Situated in the Vindhan mountain range in the centre of Madhya Pradesh, Bandhavgarh National Park is on the rail route Katni-Bilsapur, and can also be reached from Khajuraho by road (five hours). Tiger may be seen plus a wide variety of game and bird life. The best time to visit is between October and May, though in May the temperature will be very hot indeed.

Periyar (Kerala)

A captivating place, this park is accessible from Cochin, Madurai or Tirunelveli by train, or by bus from Trivandrum or Kottayam. The sanctuary is 800 sq. km (308 sq. miles) of graceful scenery set around an artificial lake from which branch secretive backwaters running deeply through jungle. Motorboats carry visitors across the lake or along the backwaters to points for viewing. The best time for observing wild life is in the early morning and again at evening time, or at feeding times. November to March is the best season and of all the wild life sanctuaries to which you might go and not see a thing, here, at Periyar, it does not matter. It is all so beautiful and seductive that actually seeing the animals is not important. Look out for birds, though; here you will see the paradise fly catcher, the male of which has a forked tail that is like a long white ribbon, over 30 cm (12 in) long, splitting and curving towards the end.

Healthy travel

A good start to trouble-free travel in India is not to start with the conviction that you will be ill!

Thousands upon thousands of Indians live their lives suffering only minor illnesses; but just as anywhere else in the world, there are times when illness does occur and if it happens to you, then there are plenty of good Indian doctors around.

Don't, therefore, arm yourself with half the contents of a chemist's shop. Take only those medicines that have been prescribed by your doctor for any permanent or temporary abnormality – blood pressure tablets, for instance, or tablets for a heart complaint.

A debilitating and all too common indisposition for a tourist is an upset stomach; for stomach-ache, diarrhoea and vomiting the treatment is easy, swift, safe and sure. It is most likely, if you are travelling with a group tour, that the tour leader will have a supply of tablets that will alleviate the symptoms. If this is not the case, then remedies such as Lomotol, Imodium or Thalazol will be quick and effective and are readily available. For any ailment, beware of drugs containing sulphur as you may be allergic to them and thereby make matters far worse.

It is better to let the body itself deal with these problems but on a holiday time will be of the essence and such a natural healing cannot be allowed for. Take curd and rice and bananas only, with a little sugar added and a pinch of salt. Drink plenty of water that has been boiled or that you know is pure (see under Water).

Malaria
Malaria is at all costs to be prevented and tablets that have been recommended by your doctor should be taken according to the instructions. Daraprim is a good weekly tablet, or pellet, and has no side effects.

Malaria is spread by the mosquito which, before puncturing the skin and sucking the blood, will probably have alighted among filthy conditions. It is important, therefore, to remember to take the tablets regularly on the same day of each week, to start taking them three weeks before leaving for India and to continue taking them for a further three weeks after returning home. Remember that malaria can be a killer.

Rabies
Rabies is widespread throughout India, and animals, even domestic ones, and especially monkeys, should be discouraged from getting too close. A dog will slink away if you just bend and pretend to be throwing a stone at it. Monkeys nearby temples should not be fed. Temples are a favourite place for both monkeys and the nut-vendors who will plead with you to feed 'the Holy Monkey' (Hanuman, the Monkey God in the Hindu pantheon of gods). There will be plenty who will feed them, so let them, and stand back and watch.

The treatment for rabies by a series of injections is unpleasant, to say the least, but it must be carried out if you have the least suspicion that you have been bitten, even by the most friendly domestic animal. New treatment is being researched all the time and injections against rabies are now available before leaving for India. The thing is – not to run the risk.

Polio
It is a wise precaution to ask your doctor for a dose of polio vaccine before leaving for India. If you have had one recently, then ask for a booster; it lasts for five years and will prevent what could be a frightful illness.

Infectious hepatitis
Though a gamma globulin injection is not proof against this infection, it is a wise precaution to have one and will certainly help to protect you, especially for a short stay. Gamma globulin is decreasingly effective over a period of six months. There are no side effects from this injection, which is usually given in the buttocks.

Water

Do not drink water anywhere other than recognized hotels, the homes of friends and in municipally safe areas. In these places water will have been treated by filtration and in some cases it will have been boiled. Boiling is always a good safeguard.

Seritabs, a preparation available on the Indian market, are tablets which render water absolutely safe for drinking. One tablet should be put into 3 litres ($5\frac{1}{4}$ pts) of water (the equivalent of four squash bottles) and left for half an hour by which time the water will be ready for drinking.

It is essential to drink plenty of water as your body will need it, and mineral waters, soda water and all the soft drinks that are available are not a substitute. Tea without milk is always good and it will be safe. *Always travel with a supply of your own drinking water.*

Dehydration can happen insidiously and you may not realize it; it is at this time that the body's system is most vulnerable. Salt intake is important but it comes in sufficient quantities in Indian food. If, however, you go on a rigorous trek or climb, then you may suffer from a faint feeling and your legs will feel unable to support you. As salt is unpalatable to eat raw and can be an emetic, salt tablets are available. They release salt into the system slowly and after half an hour's rest these symptoms will have disappeared. A good pick-me-up after dehydration is Electral Powder. Perspiring, diarrhoea, vomiting and exertions such as car driving or athletics are causes of dehydration, and Electral Powder replaces, in a palatable form – that of an orangey drink – minerals such as calcium, potassium, magnesium, sodium chloride, etc., the lack of which will cause muscle weakness, stiff neck and listlessness.

If you suffer from high blood pressure, then salt tablets must be advised by a doctor.

Doctors, dentists and chiropody

Good doctors are available throughout India but medical consultation is not free. It is wise, therefore, to ask the charge for treatment, after consultation, so that you are prepared for the account. You will be expected to pay for the consultation.

Teeth should be checked before leaving for India. There seem not to be as many good dentists as there are doctors. Indians simply have marvellous teeth which they clean assiduously twice daily (oddly enough, before meals) from cradle to grave so that they hardly need to visit a dentist. A doctor or the hotel reception will put a visitor in touch with a dentist who will be acceptable to a Westerner. You will not have to go to one of the blood-and-guts pavement dentists often seen displaying enormous and revolting-looking false teeth, rusty extractors and strange herbal filling agents.

Foot care can be obtained only in the large cities but even there chiropody is not common. The Indians' feet seem to be as indestructible as their teeth! From an early age Indians of all classes are accustomed to walking barefoot at some time or other of the day. Indeed, for most it is more comfortable than wearing sandals.

Take a sensible pair of shoes with you but leave room in your baggage for an extra pair, one that you have bought in an Indian shop. You will be surprised at their relatively low cost and their comfort. Apart from party occasions, high heels are not advised.

Walking barefoot, especially around religious buildings, can cause all manner of foot ailments, the most frequent and lasting being athlete's foot. Always wear socks – they are acceptable to both temple and mosque and serve two purposes: they protect against disease and they protect against the heat of the sun on stone and marble.

Mosquito bites

Only a few mosquito bites are malarial. The number of varieties in India, though, is seemingly uncountable and the taking of a suitable prophylactic is essential. The swelling, accompanied by a red mark of varying intensity, will last for five days no matter what ointment is applied. Ointment will, at best, only alleviate the itching. A good anaesthetic cream or gel will ease the itching and certainly stop you scratching. These bites seem not to show on Indians, but they get bitten just as much as others.

Prevention is another help. Sleep under a mosquito net where necessary if the room is not air-conditioned. Keep doors and windows shut between the hours of dawn and nine in the morning and again from four to eight in the evening. These are the times when mosquitoes are most active. Apply one of the proprietory repellants. Odomos is available all over India; oil of citron is good, but the most pleasant is oil of lavender, unavailable in India but obtainable in the West. Dab on the ankles, wrists, neck and through the hair, and it will repel them.

Sensible eating and drinking

For the visitor to India perhaps the most persistent worry will be whether or not the spices in the food will upset the stomach and, if one does not like curry, what there will be to eat.

If you fear the former, then with a little understanding and caution you will be able to relish the exciting menus that are prepared. If your fears are, though, that you really do not like curry (presuming that you have tasted curry – some people are prejudiced by the thought, not the deed), then there are many alternatives available either by asking the tour manager or the hotel reception. There is no need to eat spicy food in India, for 'boily-food', as the cook will refer to unspiced food, will always be available, since many Indians themselves eat this. Better, therefore, to order 'boily-food' if you are deterred by spices.

There are four basic rules which should be remembered:

Do not drink any water unless from a reputable hotel

Do not add any ice to anything
Do not eat any ice-cream
Do not eat any fresh fruit which you yourself have not peeled

If you follow these injunctions, then your stomach will almost certainly be fine. In good hotels the water will have been purified. The water in the container in your room will be quite pure, as will the water at the dining-table. *Do not drink from a tap*. Any water anywhere outside the hotel will be suspect; although you may see Indians drinking it, many seem immune to all impurities. Buy a plastic water bottle and fill it from the hotel water supply and never travel anywhere without it; you must have your own supply of water wherever you go. If this is practicably impossible for some reason, then drink only a reputable sealed soft drink or soda water. I caution *sealed* because it is not beyond the hundreds of child-vendors of soft drinks to refill old bottles, jam on a metal cap, and sell it as new! Never buy drinks that are in the bottles with the marbles in the top. Not only will the seal be imperfect but the 'coloured drink' inside will be suspect.

For a short stay in India, avoid all ice unless you are a guest in a private house. Ice-cream is very tempting in a hot climate and is consumed by the ton by Indians. Only that of a reputable maker, or served at the hotel, would be safe. Do not buy from a street vendor.

Bananas are, perhaps, the most ubiquitous fruit in India. They are good for the stomach and come ready-wrapped, so to speak. Oranges are the same; they, too, can be peeled and will quench the thirst. Limes are plentiful and cheap all over India and can be squeezed into soda water or pure water, adding a little sugar and a pinch of salt. All other fruit-
– dates, sultanas, plums, and especially grapes, apples and melon slices should be avoided.

Indian cooking skills have been handed down from mother to daughter, father to son, and from cook to cook, and each community or sect will have its own traditions. All over India a variety of cooking will be found that has evolved over the centuries, influenced by the traditions of Hindu, Muslim, Christian, Parsee, Sikh and European.

The cow is sacred to the Hindu, for whom it is an anathema to think of it as food. For the Muslim, the pig is despicable and similarly shunned. Whilst not all Hindus are orthodox, most Muslims are. The Christians will eat any kind of meat, but abattoirs in India are the prerogative of one sect and are places often primitive and not controlled by the health authorities. Vegetarian food, therefore, is a natural alternative.

Vegetarian food in India is very different from the Western idea and has no overtones of slimming or of necessarily being better for you. From a dietary point of view, it can sometimes be so rich as to produce obesity. This state of 'largeness' is attractive to Indians and there are many really large people who live entirely on vegetarian food, some not even eating eggs.

Meat is tenderized and cooked in spices and in yoghurt or juices and is presented in an endless variety of ways, the same meat source being used. A clever cook can transform the toughest old goat-meat into something delectable. Lamb or mutton on a menu will nearly always mean goat. Pork can be had but is eaten by relatively few people. Wild pig roam around many parts of India and will be eaten in the Punjab.

Apart from Western-type hotels, which are in the minority, all food in India is served on a metal plate or a *thali*. The latter is a flat metal dish most often made from stainless steel. On this will be put small stainless steel bowls into which are put the various vegetables and chutneys, the rice being served directly on to the thali. It may not be out of place here to repeat the old adage 'Eat till your stomach is three-quarters full and leave a quarter for the Lord', as the waiters will come round and refill the bowls again and again, also replenishing the rice, and you will eat until you burst!

A change from water to drink is *nimboo pani*, literally, lime-water. It will be served with sugar and a pinch of salt and goes well with curry – but remember, *no ice*.

I ought to explain why I emphasize no ice. Throughout India there are ice factories which turn out ice in huge quantities. The water from which the ice is made may be quite pure and filtered by the local authority. It is what happens to the ice on the way from the factory to the consumer that makes it so dangerous. The blocks of ice are transported on hand-carts or by rickshaw or even by bullock cart and the ice is broken up on the street or the filthy pavement. Often it is wrapped in gunny sacking so that a passer-by would not realize that the contents are ice; until, that is, one sees the sacking ripped open and the ice dragged through the dust to where it will be cut into manageable sizes and then used by street vendors, small hotels and the like.

Not all ice comes from the ice factory. Much is made under hygienic conditions by hotels and especially those in the upper price bracket who cater for the foreign visitor. Tours, though, often mingle hotels in order to cut costs, and whereas 'night one' may be spent in luxury, 'night two' might be in a slightly down-grade hotel, and in these lesser hotels the ice could be contaminated and therefore it is better to steer clear of it.

It is not necessary for a curry to be spice-hot. In fact, mild curries are found more often than the fiercely hot ones. Basically, southern cooking will be hotter with chillies than northern cooking, and there will also be more vegetarianism in the south. Tandoori will also not be hot, neither will Kashmiri. This does not mean that it will not be spicy; it will be, and deliciously so. If, when ordering a meal, you are wary of the taste ask the waiter to bring you a sample of the sauce – they might call it the 'gravy' – and then you will know if you are going to enjoy it.

Alcoholic drinks are available in India except in those States which have been declared 'dry'. Liquor is expensive, especially imported whisky, but India makes quite acceptable whisky (though maybe not to a Scotsman) and very good vodka and gin. Indian brandy would be best left in the shop, and the increasing number of 'imitation' fortified wines, too, would not please any but the compulsive toper, and they are foolishly expensive. Indian table wines tend to be thick and sweet, rather like a spiced sherry. Indian beer is good and is the safest and most quenching of drinks. If spirits are consumed, then do so the tropical way: dilute the spirit; this way the alcohol enters the blood stream more slowly and will not produce bad after-effects. On the whole, the soft drinks of India are the safest and best drinks and are available all over the country, and to make soda water more palatable there are all manner of bottles of squash, mango being the most exotic. Ruafsa is a pink cordial-syrup enjoyed by the Muslims and, when added to water, makes an exotic alternative. Also, there are plenty of tinned juices, such as apple and orange and mango. For emergency situations, when you are stuck somewhere without liquid, then apart from chewing a stone (not advisable), keep in the corner of your pocket or handbag a few cloves or cardamon or a little stick of cinnamon. It will be something to chew on until you reach the bar!

Photography

For colour slide photography it is good advice to take the best camera you can afford. Conditions in India vary so much, especially if one is touring extensively, that there may be need of the more sophisticated type of camera – one on which both speed and aperture can be adjusted. For snapshots, a standard instamatic camera will be adequate. Buy your film before you leave for India.

The prevailing sun and the quality of the air are the main factors to be considered. Circumstances can be deceptive and the more adjustments of which a camera is capable, the better. It is not always a guarantee of good slides or photographs to have an automatic camera, as these often have average correlations that will not take into account such factors as air pollution, refracted sunlight, dust in the atmosphere or, most of all, the angle of the sun. From around 10.30am to 4.30pm the sun will be overhead, causing strong downward light, and this light gives an intense glare on horizontal planes and deep shadow on vertical ones. A camera that is capable of manual control is, therefore, more useful. Some of the most desirable scenes will present themselves as perfect pictures at moments only possible for photographing by manual adjustment of your camera.

Look carefully at the prevailing conditions. You may be in the dry desert of Rajasthan or in the humid south where the air is full of invisible water droplets which produce a fog-like effect. In contrast, there is the clear air of the hill stations and the deceptively bright light among the snows of the Himalayas. Such differing conditions need constant readjustment of the camera, and a fixed ultra-violet filter and a lens hood are desirable.

There are countless developing shops in India which will process black

21 Photograph taken with light directly overhead at Bhubeneshwar, Orissa

and white films adequately. They give a cheap and speedy service and to have a test film developed and printed during the first days in India will provide a useful guide to show if you are doing the right thing. Colour film processing is not so readily available; the only reliable laboratories for slide processing are in Delhi and Bombay and the time taken for processing a film might be longer than your stay. Better to wait and have colour film, especially transparencies, processed in the West.

Remember to check the expiry date on your films before leaving, as deterioration accelerates faster in a hot climate.

Buy a security protection bag, usually made of lead foil, in which to keep both used and unused film. All airports have different methods of checking hand baggage and while you will be assured by the operators that X-ray machines and scanners will not harm film, they might. Though the protection bags are not claimed to be fully proof against misadventure, if you use one you will have the satisfaction of knowing that you have taken the precaution. Never put exposed or unexposed film in baggage that will not be accompanying you.

IV Flora and Fauna

Trees

It does not seem to matter at which season you visit India, the trees will be in leaf and many will probably be in flower.

Apart from the very north of the country there is a continuance of leaf-replacement – the re-leafing after leaf-drop – that is often so rapid that it seems as if India is a country of evergreens!

The pipal, for instance, will shed its thousands upon thousands of leaves within a week and at the same time young leaves will be sprouting from its branches. It is at this time that the pipal is most attractive. The young leaves appear first as a peach colour which deepens to pale copper until finally they swell to a brilliantly shining lime-green colour.

As one travels throughout the country, certain species stand out familiarly, trees that one reads about in books. The palm is an obvious one, being a reminder of southern seaside towns of Europe and of hot-houses around the world. The banyan is another and is to be seen everywhere, its dull dark-green leaves on rather haphazard branches and its twigs flopping in the breeze around its aerial roots.

The palm and the banyan are easy to recognize but other trees may be less so, and, in the hope that travellers will come to recognize more species, the list that follows is of those trees that are most likely to be seen either from the train or bus window, or when walking in the country, or around towns and cities.

Urban planting of trees has been a continuous civic activity over the centuries and is, nowadays, with the world's awareness of the need for conservation and protection, a part of the budgeting of States throughout India.

One good reason for planting a tree is the shade it gives, and nowhere is the respite from the broiling sun more appreciated than in the city streets. Here you will see the larger, spreading trees such as the banyan, the neem, the gul mohur and the spathodia. They may be planted in avenues or as groups, their bases forming islands for tiny businesses like that of a cigarette seller or a snack stall, and often this rooty interruption in a pavement becomes the temporary 'home' for displaced persons.

Countryside planting is mostly for the crop yielded by the tree.

Tamarind is a favourite and so is the mango and the palm, especially the coconut palm. One mature coconut tree will, over the years, yield three rupees a day to the owner who will sell the coconuts, their fibre, the leaves, the bark and, eventually, the trunk; and three rupees daily will keep a family of four from starving in the south of India.

In the country are the really ancient trees of India, but alas they are ill-treated by vandals seeking fire-wood and, due to this constant despoliation, thousands of the trees have grown mis-shapen and grotesque. The best specimens are to be found in the many botanical gardens around India, or on private estates. The baobab, to name but one, was introduced into India from Africa. One baobab tree is on record as existing for over 5,000 years! A really ancient specimen can be seen at Bijapur in Karnataka State.

A tree now frequently seen in India, but a native of Australia, is the eucalyptus. It has adapted well over the sub-continent and adds a lacey gracefulness to aerial views, and its bluish colour relieves the green in a cool way.

But a fuller description of just one tree will give some idea of the extraordinary benificence of nature and how this has been taken advantage of by man to produce an abundance of riches.

The mowha or the Indian butter tree

This is one of the most important forest trees of India, not because of its wood but because of its flowers and fruit.

It was named after Fernando Bassia, once curator of the Botanical Gardens at Bologna, *Bassia latifolia*.

It is a large tree, having thick grey bark that is cracked and crinkled. From February to April, after leaf-fall, sickly-scented clusters of flowers hang from branchlets. The flowers are mainly white but have a flush of pink. New leaves sprout while the tree flowers, the effect being freshly beautiful.

The gathering of the edible flowers is important to all country and hill people. Daily the flowers drop in abundance and are swept up by proprietorial families who will have slept nearby, guarding their 'crop'. The flowers, after pressing and preserving, taste like figs. A strong spiritous drink is made from them – a drink that has the misfortune to have a bad smell! When the tree fruits, all the parts of the berries are used. The outer coat is eaten as a vegetable, the inner coat ground to flour, and the kernel pressed to yield a thick, yellow oil, hence the name, Indian butter tree. The 'butter' is especially used in cooking by the jungle tribes, or is used in soap and candle making.

Medicinally, too, the tree provides plenty. It gives from its bark a relief for leprosy; the flower juice cures coughs and sickness and heart trouble, whilst the fruit is used in cases of consumption and diseases of the blood. The tree's sap is prepared and used to relieve rheumatism.

Whatever is left over of the tree's bounty is made into valuable field manure. It is altogether a useful tree, to say nothing of its ample shade. It grows wide and strong and can be seen all over central India – at the 'Undying Banyan Tree' at Allahabad, near Khajaraho, at Benares and all over Uttar Pradesh and Madhya Pradesh.

You need to be in India in April to really experience its cloying perfume and see the harvesting of its yield, but in early March, just before leaf-fall, the whole tree turns gold.

There are many exotic specimens of trees and those travellers who wish to know more about them would be well advised to obtain a copy of *100 Beautiful Trees of India*, by Charles McCann. This is well illustrated in colour and is published by Taraporevala, Bombay.

Here are some of the trees that will be rewarding to identify. The blue-flowering jacaranda (April–June), scented like the hyacinth; the mango, pungently scented through mid-March to mid-April; the frangipani, scented like vanilla ice-cream and seen around temples – hence its name, the temple tree; the bauhinia, tall and rounded, bears a profusion of sweetly scented flowers that look like miniature orchids – the flowers can be picked and dipped in batter and eaten as a rather exotic snack!

The cassia, or Indian laburnum, as its name suggests, is hung with bright yellow racemes. The silk cotton tree, tall and erect with angular, spokey branches of a greyish colour, is, when flowering, an exuberant sight. The gliricidia is a smallish tree which flowers in February-time. The flowers are similar to those of the pea and they attract many birds, one of which is the golden oriel. Millingtonia, or Indian cork tree, is a tall tree which bears thousands of highly-scented thin white trumpet-shaped flowers. They smell like nutmeg. You will not notice this tree at first, only the sweet scent in the air, but if you look on the ground, you will see the fallen white flowers in profusion and know that you are under a millingtonia.

The rain tree is a large, spreading tree with black bark and pale green foliage. It bears flowers which resemble the flame of old gas-burners, dainty, feathery things which detach themselves and float down as seed.

The Jerusalem thorn, called also Parkinsonia after John Parkinson (1567–1650), a British herbalist, is unusual in that the trunk is smooth and green. It has pine-like leaves and bright yellow flowers. Beware of the thorns – they can tear flesh and clothing with ease!

The water pistol tree, botanically known as *Spathodia*, has large vermillion flowers that hold water. When they fall, children pick them up and squirt the juice at each other, hence the nickname. The casurina, a wispy, leggy tree, grey-green in colour, is often seen by the coast as it adapts well there and is useful to stop erosion. The wood is used for making fine charcoal. Lignum vitae is a rare tree but can be seen by the traveller. There are some in the gardens at the Theosophical Society's headquarters in Madras. The flowers are bright blue and the wood extremely hard. It is from the wood of the lignum vitae that bowls are made, the type which spin over the bowling greens of the world. Palms come in many varieties; the coconut palm, the tall palmyra palm and the areca-nut palm are three commonly seen.

Of all the trees, the neem tree might be said to be of the most use to the most people in India, and it is copiously planted. It it a large tree which bears sweetly scented flowers. Its gum is used in Ayurvedic medicine as an antiseptic and it is also used in the manufacture of soap. Its green twigs are used for cleaning the teeth and its oil is added to toothpaste; a wine is prepared from its bark and its flowers mixed in curry add a health-giving piquancy.

Lastly, the tamarind, seen often singly or in clumps across fields gives much welcome shade to field labourers. Without the fruit of the tamarind, Indian cooking would be lacking in a cardinal ingredient – the lemony juice from the tamarind seed pod. The tamarind gets its name from the Persian 'Tamar-i-Hindi', which means 'Indian date'. The husks of the seeds have been used as road surfacing and the seeds ground and made into jungle bread.

Shrubs

There are many shrubs growing in India which will be familiar to those who have travelled around the Mediterranean regions, though in India these seem to be more refulgent and exotic, perhaps because of the often romantically oriental background.

Oleander is seen frequently, either as a hedge plant or as a free-standing bush. It has fragrant pink and white flowers and seems always to be in bloom. Its graceful charm, though, is deceiving, as all parts of the plant are poisonous. This danger is one of the reasons that it flourishes so well, for cattle and goats will not eat it and it is seldom picked for the house. In some parts of India its hollow stems are fashioned into hookah pipes.

Lantana is another shrub easily recognized, growing as it does all over the south of France, Italy and Spain. It is really a weed and has become a scourge in India as it takes over arable land, spreading amazingly quickly. Its seeds are cast by birds, who are partial to its green or blue-black fruit.

Hibiscus needs little introduction, though in India many different varieties will be seen of every colour imaginable. The flowers are exotic indeed, hanging like huge bells with their pollen-laden 'tongues' protruding. The double ones are so full of petals that they droop.

Poinsettia is the last familiar one to mention; it is associated in the West with Christmas but in India it grows like a weed. Originally from Mexico and named after Admiral Poinsett of South Carolina who originally cultivated the plant, there are now many varieties. In India magnificent hedges of it can be seen. The plant is poisonous, exuding a white sap, and care should be taken not to allow this to rub off onto the skin. The yellow flowers are particularly radiant.

Some unfamiliar shrubs, but ones which will be seen wherever there has been municipal planting, for instance, are:

Daranta, or golden dewdrop. Planted as hedges, its purple bracts are most attractive. They smell similar to heliotrope and contrast well with the dark green foliage. Yellow fruits may be seen at the same time as the flowers.

Camphire: a commonly seen Indian shrub. Another name is henna – the name of the well-known copper-coloured dye. Favoured by Muslims, especially those who have journeyed to Mecca, henna is a popular hair dye and is non-permanent. The colour comes from a paste made from the leaves of the camphire. It is a straggly, prickly plant which bears spires of creamy flowers which are very fragrant.

Gardenia. Two forms of gardenia can be seen, the small-flowering *florida* and the large white *lucida*. The latter is more noticeable, its large waxy flowers showing off well and attracting, too, with their heady perfume. The gardenia is found in dry areas such as the Deccan and south-central India.

Yellow oleander. A variety of the more usual pink-white oleander, this yellow form is free-flowering, has the same leaf-shape and is unmistakable. Its trumpet-like flowers have a faint fragrance.

Yellow elder. Its leaves are typical of the elder family. It is fragrant and its yellow foxglove-like flowers hang in clusters. In gardening catalogues this plant is listed under *Tecoma*.

Nytanthes, or tree of sorrow. Planted often as a hedge, its name comes from its flowering mostly at night and thus its association with death. It makes a good bush and is seen around temples, its flowers being offered to the gods. The flowers are creamy-white and scented.

Poinciana, or Barbados pride. A better name, and one used most frequently in India is the peacock flower. It grows up to 3 m (10 ft) high, has feathery leaves and exuberant spires of gorgeous blooms radiating from a central stem. The buds open pale yellow and turn vermilion and, from a distance, look like fire. Many are to be seen at Khajuraho from February onwards. Ink is made from the burnt wood of the peacock flower and, rather suitable from so fiery-looking a plant, the leaves are an effective purgative!

Ervatamia, or tageri in south India and tagar in the north. Colloquially named moonbeam plant, this invariably grows near temples and palaces and shrines. It is an evergreen plant which bears a profusion of white wax-like flowers, large or small according to variety. The scent is delicate and women like to bind the flower buds in their hair. The shrub can be recognized by its dark green foliage and dazzlingly white flowers which show up starkly in the moonlight. A perfumed oil is extracted from its wood, the wood being also burned as incense.

Climbing plants

No visitor to India could miss the many varieties of climbing plants that spill over roof-tops or climb up trellis and pergola or just ramble around tree trunks.

There is an old adage, rather cynical, really, that a doctor may bury his mistakes but an architect can only cover his over with creepers. One could wish, though, that more architects did cover their pre-stressed concrete with creepers and climbers, for India is fast becoming a concrete jungle and less of a natural one.

Some climbers are grown only for their foliage. One thinks of the ivy, common in northern India. Another is the *Monstre deliciosa*, often seen as a pot plant in Western houses. In India it will cover a sizeable tree trunk with its enormous leaves, leaves which have holes in them and give the plant the nickname Swiss cheese plant, after the Gruyere cheese.

Another climber grown for its leaves is the asparagus, commonly seen in the cooler regions. This climbing variety of the garden vegetable sends up feathery fronds and looks most beautiful draped over time-mellowed bungalow porches.

Listed below in alphabetical order are those climbers that you are most likely to see and be able to identify.

Antigonon. This climber, often called the Sandwich Island Creeper, can be seen covering railway fences, trellises and really large trees. It also makes a delightful hedging if kept under control. It throws out sprays of tiny white and pink flowers continuously from the end of the monsoon period, and has a second flowering in the wintertime, ie December, January and February.

Beaumontia grandiflora is a large evergreen shrubby climber which is often called the Nepal trumpet climber. It has large lily-like flowers and from a distance looks rather like a rhododendron. The flowers are trumpet-shaped and have a slight fragrance, similar to vanilla. It is a showy plant, is a native of eastern India and has spread all over the country. It flowers from November to March.

The bignonias. This species includes some of the most gorgeous flowering climbers to be seen in India. Yellow, purple or red, their tubular flowers agglomerate to mask all sign of leaves. They can be seen on walls or pergolas in private gardens and in botanical gardens. The most brilliant is the pyrostegia, well-named for its fire-coloured flowers.

Bougainvillea was originally a native of South America. It is the most spectacular and ubiquitously planted climber in India. It can be seen in a bewildering number of named varieties and in almost countless colours. One place to see many of the differing colours is in the nursery garden of the Taj Mahal, at Agra. This garden is to the left of the main gateway and is seldom seen, so tucked away is it, and so hasty are the visitors. Another place to see varieties of bougainvillea is at the Lal Bagh, the botanical gardens at Bangalore. Here there is a special nursery which raises all varieties, and it is a change to see colours other than the familiar Mediterranean magenta. Here there are cream and buff and brown varieties and peach, too, and a deep apricot.

Perhaps the most striking of all bougainvilleas is the iridescently colourful variety called Mary Palmer, a shifting spectacle of cerise and white sepals, its double colour and fulsome blooming making it a firm favourite.

Bougainvillea has one thing lacking, and that is scent. Were it to have this added attraction, then it would be the most perfect climber as it never seems to stop blooming and it loves the hot season.

Some varieties are: Aida – rose madder; Jubilee – terra-cotta-orange; Maharajah of Mysore – pale rose; Tomato Red – orange-carmine; Snow White – paper-white; Golden Queen – orange-yellow; Lady Mary Baring – gold; Princess Margaret Rose – magenta rose; and, of course, Mary Palmer.

Clerodendrum spendens. This species produces flowers of incredible beauty in such profusion as almost to hide its dark green leaves. The flowers are a dazzling crimson with a touch of orange, and a good specimen will cover quite a large wall. They should not be confused with the bignonias. The latter are more 'yellowy' and the flowers are in large trusses.

Jacquemontia is a twining plant and a favourite for screening purposes as the growth is dense and the flowering season perpetual. The flowers are bell-shaped, of a beautiful ultramarine blue, with a white eye, and they are profuse.

Petrea volubilis – the purple wreath – is a beautiful light mauve-blue shrubby climber. It flowers on the plains of northern India from February to April. It has a hyacinth-like perfume and grey bark against which the flowers show off to advantage.

Quisqualis indica. Better known as the Rangoon Creeper, this climber has tubular flowers which start white and turn gradually pink and then orange. The climber gives out a fresh scent similar to that of the lime tree blossom of Europe. The flowers are in incredible numbers, borne in trusses, and are set off admirably by the mid-green foliage. The climber reaches to a considerable height and, whilst perfuming a garden the whole day long, it is at night that the perfume increases. It is never cloying, always refreshing, and will make the hottest night seem cool.

Thunbergia grandiflora can be seen in hot-houses all over the world. There is a splendid one at Kew. The flowers are Cambridge blue touched with white and yellow and they hang in racemes, the flowers shaped like Canterbury bells or foxgloves; they are trumpet-shaped but curved and very dainty.

A relative of *Thunbergia* is grown in European gardens both in the soil and in pots. It is called black-eyed Susan.

Of the ipomea (morning glory) and the jasmine, honeysuckle, rose and wisteria nothing special here need be said other than to mention that they are part of India's flora and will be easily identifiable.

A special mention must be made, though, of the banksia climbing roses that are to be seen in Kashmir during May and June. They form cream mountains of dense, scented flowers, and are a memorable sight.

Birds

It is not possible to be in India for very long without noticing, either by sight or by song, the many birds on the ground, in the trees and in the air; they seem to be everywhere. Large or small, visible or hidden, they command attention – sometimes by their brilliant colouring, sometimes by their sheer size and often, like starlings in England, by their number.

Birds in India are protected to an extent by the Hindu respect for life and it could be because of this that they fear man less and are therefore easier to spot.

Many thousands of birds, though, are trapped by one method or another and are sold as caged birds – a very lucrative trade.

Bird markets are noisy places full of captured song birds. There will be hundreds of parakeets and finches, hill mynas – birds which imitate man so well – and even owls, which are thought of as mysterious and are used in magic ritual. A questionable virtue of these places is that there you will see species which are difficult to see in the wild.

Here are some birds that you will most certainly see during a visit to India:

Egrets. Perhaps the cattle egret is the first bird that will attract the attention of a visitor. This quite white and fairly large bird travels with cattle, often the buffalo, riding on the back of, or scuttling underneath, the animal, seizing the insects started up by the animal's movements. These egrets are also seen roosting in rice fields and their pure whiteness stands out against the intense green of the young rice.

Vultures. The Bengal vulture, seen throughout India, is as large as a peacock, as, too, is the king vulture. The former is mostly brown whilst the latter has a red neck and legs. Vultures eat carrion, and large gatherings collect at animal carcases which, no matter how big, they devour with incredible speed. Repulsive when grounded, vultures are most graceful in flight.

Eagles and kites. There are numerous eagles to be seen; the tawny eagle, the crested serpent eagle, the short-toed eagle are only some of the names. They are often shy of man and inhabit somewhat inaccessible places. Easier to see is the kestrel, by small rivers and water ways or near to stony river beds.

The Pariah kite is a large dark brown bird, nearly as big as a vulture, and is often seen wheeling on air currents. The Brahminy kite is large and is beautiful in flight. It is chestnut-coloured with white markings. It is seen over ports and islands and large water ways. Watch for them from the Esplanade outside the Taj Mahal Hotel in Bombay or from Elephanta Island in Bombay Harbour.

Peacocks. Gone are the days when this exotic bird was served as the main course, complete with tail feathers. It is very much protected, not only by law but by the feelings of the people. Apart from it being the national bird of India it is a holy bird and part of Hindu mythology. If you are visiting Gwalior, hundreds can be seen roosting on the battlements there, gliding at times into the gorges that surround the fort. But the peacock is really a ubiquitous bird and is commonly found in most areas, though perhaps less so in the south.

The Sarus crane is easily spotted, if only because of its size: it stands 1.5 m (5 ft) tall and is, indeed, striking when seen across fields, often being mistaken for a person. They are grey birds with bare red legs and a bare red head. They are said to mate for life, a fact which has appealed to the sentimental side of man's nature, and in consequence the birds have been protected and are surprisingly tame.

Red wattled lapwing. A familiar member of the plover family, this bird is a common sight. Its call is said to resemble 'did-he-do-it', but I have yet to identify the shrieking it makes as being anything like that. It is seen around puddles and small lakes and forest glades. It is the size of a partridge, has a brown back, white below, with crimson wattles by each eye, and has yellow legs.

Crow pheasant is a handsome, proud and cruel bird. Larger than a crow, it eats the young of other birds. It has bright chestnut wings and flops around the bottoms of hedges pecking for insects.

Barbet. Grass-green with crimson breast, yellow throat and green under-parts, this is a small bird, difficult to spot but not difficult to hear. It is nicknamed the coppersmith bird because of its incessant call which resembles the beating of copper.

Hoopoe. A fawn bird with black and white bars marking the wings, back and tail, it has a conspicuous crest on the head. The bill is curved and long, used for probing into lawns for leather-jackets and other larvae.

Blue jay. One of the most gorgeous birds and the size of a pigeon, it is described by India's foremost ornithologist, Salim Ali, as being Oxford and Cambridge blue. Its breast is a dusky-peach colour. When it flies its wings form huge blue fans.

Green bee eater is a small bird, and most colourful; it perches on wires, and flies off catching insects – and bees if there are any. Bright green with a rufous head and a characteristic long pointed tail.

Black drongo is a small, crow-sized bird, jet black and slim, with deeply forked long tail. Seen everywhere, often in the territory of the blue jay.

Golden oriel is a largish, bright golden-yellow bird with black wings and tail. It is hard to see amongst the leaves as it is a shy bird but well worth watching for at the tops of trees near gardens. To see one is an unforgettable experience.

Mynas. These happy, squabbling birds are all over the place. They move in noisy colonies and have an annoying habit of imitating other birds, thus confusing the bird spotter.

There are many different species of myna: the pied myna, as the name suggests, is black and white; the Brahminy myna is pinkish and brown, but the most common to be seen is the common Indian myna, which has yellow eyes and legs and white flashes on a rufous body.

Red vented bulbul is a smokey-brown bird with a distinguishing red vent under the tail. It has a cheery crest and hops among the lower branches of trees and shrubs, and is seen everywhere.

The list of birds to be seen is endless but some others that you might see are: kingfishers, hornbills, finches, woodpeckers, yellow wagtails, buntings, red starts, cuckoos, weaver birds and sunbirds. The latter are tiny birds which hover before the flowers of trees and climbers, probing deep into the flowers for the nectar. The purple sunbirds shine in the sun like silk shot with gold.

To know more about the birds of India, buy a copy of *The Book of Indian Birds* by Salim Ali. This is pocket-sized and has colour illustrations of all the common birds. It is published by the Bombay Natural History Society and is available at the larger bookshops.

V Entertainment

Classical Indian music

The origins of Indian music can be traced to the early scriptural writing, the Vedas, and examples of its performance can be seen in paintings and ancient temple sculptures. Its ancestry is that of legend, history and of symbolic meanings.

The seven notes which make up the musical scale of Indian music are believed to have been revealed directly by God. The present form of Indian music has developed as a part of worship in temple and mosque.

Musical presentation of song or dance is very much *what* the artist is singing about or depicting by dance rather than how good, or otherwise, is the performance. The story is more important than the artist; it is the song, not the singer, and the dance, not the dancer. This discipline has led to a tradition not of prima donnas or principal dancers but of artists who dedicate themselves, singly or as a team, to their performance.

Inevitably there are artists who become so well known that their reputation is international. Their dedication, though, is more spiritual than worldly, and their performance can be sublime.

For the Westerner a signal dissimilarity between hearing Indian and Western music is the absence of harmony – Indian music being purely melodic. Melody is made up of tones and half and quarter tones which relate to each other by their continuity or repetition. Harmonic structure has no part in Indian classical music and it is because of this and the unfamiliarity of quarter tones, plus the lack of perfect pitch, that Indian music sounds strident or discordant to the Western ear.

The basic notes around which a continuing melody is imposed and on which intricate variations are woven is called a *raga*, and the rhythm of the music is called the *tala*. These two basic elements form the foundations of Indian classical music. Upon these are overlaid such refinements as style, interpretation and subtlety, the material for which is inexhaustible. There are innumerable pure septatonic ragas (meaning those that use all the seven notes of the scale) and there are many derivative ones. Over 400 ragas are classified and all are in constant use.

Some instruments used in Indian music are:

Sitar: an instrument having strings stretched along a lengthy neck which is attached to an ornamental gourd and has frets that are movable.

Vina: another stringed instrument having a double stringed board over two gourds, the whole being beautifully ornamented with tortoise-shell, mother-of-pearl and silver inlay. It is to the sitar what the clavichord is to the piano: softer, mellow and very subtle.

Tabla: a percussion instrument like a bongo drum.

Mridangam: percussion instrument with a skin on either side of an oval-shaped drum. The left hand plays one rhythm whilst the right hand another. Expert players can tell a story by the beats of the mridangam, their fingers making different nuances of sound at incredible speed.

Harmonium: a small hand organ usually three octaves in length, often seen in Christian missions. Played without harmony, it is used as a drone

Violin: the Western violin, played either under the chin, between the legs, or wherever the player finds comfortable. It is bowed without vibrato.

Santour: Eastern dulcimer instrument played by keys which pluck strings and give a twanging effect.

Flute: as the Western flute; produces the haunting sound often associated with Indian sunset scenes in travelogues. The primitive flute is that used by the snake charmers.

Tambora: a sitar-like drone instrument.

Instruments and voices in the West endeavour to use some vibrato, but no instrument or voice uses this technique in Indian music.

It is useful, perhaps, to remember that, whilst much of Indian music will sound discordant to the Western ear, so, conversely, will Western classical music seem unappealing to the ear of the average Indian. Few Indians really appreciate classical Western music, just as only a few Westerners appreciate classical Indian music.

Prejudice and dislike, on both sides, is a problem mainly of ignorance. In an effort to encourage both forms there have been attempts at synthesizing the two genres, notably by Yehudi Menuhin and Ravi Shankar and the results are charming and are enjoyed by many, though such disparate historical origins do not auger well for lasting harmony.

Indian classical dancing

The classical dance has evolved slowly, influenced by mythology, the temple and the Vedas and by both folk and tribal dancing.

Out of these four elements have developed four main classical schools of dance: Bharatnatyam, which is predominant in the south; Kathak, seen throughout northern India; Manipuri dancing, coming from the north-east, and Kathakali, practised throughout Kerala.

Older than the classical dance of temple and theatre are the dances of the people – the folk dances and the tribal dances.

The folk dances are full of spontaneity and are inseparable from the changing seasons – from rain and from hunting, marriage and death. These dances mirror the lives of the people, they tell of primordial events, and are powerful in welding the people and their culture.

There are particular dances for particular regions. In Gujarat there is the Gharba dance, in the Punjab the Bhangra, and in Rajasthan one sees Bhanjara dancing. Simple in step, repetitive in rhythm and exhausting in length, these dances are at the heart of Indian dancing.

Tribal dances are performed by India's many tribal communities. These tribals are now referred to as Adivasis, or 'original inhabitants' (of India). They live mainly in hill and forest areas and their life is little changed over the centuries.

The dances of the Adivasis are primitive in concept, expressing courage, fear, exuberance and their own particular form of animistic religion. They can be watched at Saputara (literally, the Snake Hills) in south Gujarat, which is within easy access of Bombay, Baroda and Ahmedabad.

Classical dancing tells a story by body posture, by hand gestures and by facial expression. Body postures include the various attitudes of men and women carved on temple walls. The intricate technique of Bharatnatyam was originally studied, perfected and practised by temple dancers, called Devadasis. It is not now so, but their legacy is kept alive by the many professional troupes of dancers and by the increasing numbers of amateurs.

Costume also illustrates the story of the dance. In Kerala, the Kathak-ali dancers add a complicated mask make-up. Colour and silk and jewellery enhance the dancers and provide the audience with a gorgeous spectacle. A performance of a long work like the Ramayana will take several evenings to complete. It is a fascinating and rewarding experience, made even more so by the beautiful dress of the Indian audience.

Emotion is conveyed by facial expressions which, often fleeting, are missed by Western observers, yet these expressions are a cardinal part of the dancer's art – the eyes, especially.

'Bharat' means India and 'natya' means dance, and the particular form Bharatnatyam, though mainly seen in the south, has ardent followers all over India, and it will not be difficult for the visitor to find out where performances are to be held.

Kathakali dancing is rare outside Kerala and so is the Manipuri style away from the north-east. Kathak dancing, though, is frequently per-formed in Delhi and some of the larger towns in Uttar Pradesh such as Agra and Lucknow, and also in Rajasthan. Kathak dancing is essentially for entertainment, showing off the vitality of the dancers, especially the males.

Indian classical dancing is closely linked with Hindu mythology and with the Hindu way of life. It is a reflection of the attainment of the spirit of man, of the idea of God, of the emotions of good and evil, and of nature.

The prayers and chanting that precede each performance, the garlanded god, the incense and the flowers – all are respects that emanate from the Vedas, whose teachings are rudimentary to the dance in India.

The cinema, television and video

With the production of well over 700 films on average per year (the 1983–4 figure was 740), India has become the world's largest producer. The speed with which films come off the production line is astonishing. From the 1983/4 official figures it was revealed that the Madras studios made the most films, and these, too, in the Telegu language, beating the Hindi total by two. The Telegu films numbered 134 and the Hindi films 132. After these came those made in Tamil (128), Malayam (112) and decreasingly through other regional languages down to only one made in Sanskrit.

Of the actual total of 740 films made, ten per cent had a crime background, two per cent were for children or were devotional, whilst 80 per cent, or 588 films, were on a social theme – all made, of course, into maxi or mini extravaganzas.

To the Western eye both male and female filmstars seem all to be out of the same mould. The men have a lock of hair falling over the forehead, a chubby face, and are running to fat. The women are coy, doe-eyed and voluptuous; both seem quite sexless and both are able to sing and dance.

Movie-going in India is escapism on a grand scale. An enormous audience is constantly excited and titilated by an equally constant stream of films. One can observe by their haircut and their dress how young Indian men copy one or other of their film idols.

To see on film scrawny ill-fed looking men and thin women would not please an audience which is mainly composed of millions just like that and whose daily life is punctuated by poverty, beggars and under-privilege. Film audiences in the main comprise men who wish to escape into the world of make-believe. The world of come-uppance, of marital squabbling, of brigandage and cops and robbers, and especially the rich, fat, city life of expensive Bombay flats lit by chandeliers and having grand staircases, are fine for the song and dance sequences. Ever-popular locations such as Kulu and Kashmir are places where most will never go and which for them are just a dream; and their celluloid dreams have living 'gods' – the stars – such as Shashi Kapoor and Amitabh Bachchan.

The cinema has become an obsessive passion throughout the country and the fires of this passion have been fanned by the industry's incredible profitability – a profitability equalled nowhere in the world. In India there is no alternative entertainment, or there was not until the advent of television and, latterly, the video. Both, though, are only a minor hiatus

22 Movie-going escapism. Most posters are hand-painted and, by their huge
number, form a large part of advertising street art

for the film-making moghuls and are no competition for the glamour and
excitement of going to a movie.

For the millions who have little entertainment, anything is entertain-
ing. The dancing bear, the snake charmer, the puppet show and the one-
man band can still be seen around village India, but should there be a
travelling movie show in the vicinity, then these stand little chance of an
audience.

The cinema industry is the largest entertainment medium in India and
it is the cheapest. It has been so fostered by the producers and its stars,
and so well promoted, that it would need to be a very poor film indeed
that would not recoup its costs and make a profit.

Epic follows epic with unfailing regularity and each will be seen many
times over by the eager populace. Stars are so numerous that none but a
few names are memorable to the Westerner. Super-stars become gods and
command enormous fees, profits from an audience that, at a conservative
estimate, would be in excess of 500 million.

Many stars dabble in local politics, their vote-winning potential being
obvious, and they transfer from the film world to the world of politics like
a celluloid role change.

For the millions of villagers the film is a way of escaping from their
daily toil and drudgery into the glamorous world of heroes, ancient and
modern, of comedy, and of sexuality without sex.

There are other films made in India, the so-called 'art' films such as
those of the Bengali director Satyajit Ray. These films are appreciated by
only a small audience. They do not compete with the Big Hindi Movie,
and nor are they intended to. For the Westerner, though, they are much
more acceptable entertainment, and Ray's films, in particular, enjoy a
wider appreciation outside India than even in Bengal.

The average Indian movie, in whatever regional language, contains
elements of pathos, comedy, extravaganza, song and dance, and titila-

23 The Shalimar Gardens – a typical Kashmiri film location

tion, and is garishly coloured. It is made for a known market and to deviate from this recipe is to court financial disaster. The task of re-educating so vast a public would be like trying to melt a lump of sugar on an ice-cube.

The Indian film industry does not fear outside competition; rather it welcomes it, though in comparatively small doses. The 1983/4 figures show that 124 foreign films were certified for showing throughout India.

At the time of writing, the Indian film censor is still unsure about the validity of screen kisses, and Indian actresses regard the issues as their Western counterparts regard screen nudity. This has led to the emergence of the 'indirect kiss', whereby the heroine will place her lips on an article (for example a cup), and then pass it to the hero, who touches the same place with his lips. This was considered highly erotic on its first appearance, and is now accepted as being representative of a passionate embrace. The audience can be shown luscious lips, nubile thighs and sexy belly-dancing, arguably more provocative than a kiss. You are permitted to watch rape, bride-burnings, shootings and torture, but you will not see a kiss. Such a sequence will often be cut from a foreign film unless shown at one of the film festivals. It is, of course, hypocritical, but the guarding of public morals is as contentious in India as everywhere else. Inevitably though, there are ways of getting round the present rules and eventually effecting a permanent change in the censorship laws. Foreign films shown via video will not have a little influence in bringing about change.

Television has now a permanent hold in India and is being made available to an ever-increasing audience as a continuous process, and transmissions are becoming more efficient and diverse now that India is using satellite. 'I Love Lucy' and 'Yes, Minister' are two of the popular programmes that come from other countries.

Home video is such a status symbol and is such compelling instant entertainment that few middle-class homes are now without a set. Only the more considerate will turn off a programme for a visitor; the assumption being that the visitor, also, will enjoy the showing, whatever the language! Servants and family will gather round and conversation will, if required, be at shouting pitch. The quality of picture is of little consideration. Most of the foreign VCR's are a thousand times pirate-copied and lack the colours and definition of the originals but this seems unimportant to the avid viewers.

One great problem is the actual television set. Many foreign sets are imported (a newspaper quoted in February 1985 a monthly import figure of 100,000) without guarantee or knowledge of provenance. Another problem regarding anything relying on electricity, especially in rural areas, is the fluctuating power supply which disallows good picture control.

All over India private entrepreneurs will rent a television set, a video and a couple of films, plus a room, and then show four programmes daily to paying audiences, perhaps a hundred at a time, all packed together and having paid upwards of 20 rupees each.

Naturally, the pornographic movie has not been overlooked and one is never very far from a 'domestic showing' – at a price. Remembering the ban on kissing one can only wonder what effect this accessibility to explicit sex movies will have.

VI Gazetteer

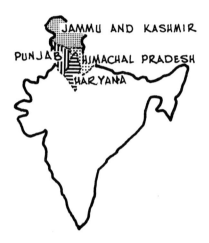

Jammu and Kashmir

One cannot compare Kashmir with any other place, in or out of India. Extravagant epithets such as 'an Oriental Switzerland' or 'an emerald set among pearls' or, most often used, 'the Venice of the mountains' do not encapsulate what it is about Kashmir that is quite unique. It is not another Lake District nor a 'Schwarzwald'; it is only Kashmir.

Kashmir is nearly as big in area as Britain and is almost wholly mountainous. The State is called Jammu and Kashmir, Jammu being the southern part nearer Delhi, to which few people go other than for business or for visiting relatives. The most spectacular part of the State is Kashmir and in particular the Vale of Kashmir. This vale, or valley, is 135 km (84 miles) in length and 32–40 km (20–25 miles) wide and is set up high in the Himalayas, 1,707 m (5600 ft) above sea level. It corresponds in latitude to Damascus or to Fez in Morocco or, surprisingly, to Atlanta in Georgia.

Francois Bernier was the first European to enter the Vale of Kashmir and he wrote, in 1665, 'In truth, the kingdom surpasses in beauty all that my warmest imagination had anticipated'. The Emperor, Jehangir, returning to Kashmir, fell ill en route and died whispering 'Kashmir, only Kashmir!'(1627).

Srinagar, the main town of Kashmir, is set on both sides of the river Jhelum and close by the waters of Lake Dal, a lake which is 8 km (5 miles) long and 3 km (2 miles) wide and which is peppered with islands and 'floating gardens' made out of intertwined roots and mud.

It is amongst this fascinating water scenery that the famous houseboats are moored. These boats were devised by the British, who wished to have a permanent escape from the heat of the plains, in Kashmir. They were, however, prevented by the ruler of Kashmir from owning land and their ingenious solution was the houseboat. Many of the original ones are still afloat and there are many new ones.

The houseboats are well furnished and spacious. Their drawing-rooms resemble the elegance of Edwardian times, with mahogany and teak furniture, wall lights, Persian carpets and pictures hung against carved pine walls. The dining-room might have a sideboard, a cabriol-legged table and chairs, chintz curtains and much well-polished silver. Bathrooms range from the antique, still with bath-tubs on claw feet and with needle showers, to the modern pastel-tiled functional room with chromium fittings and bidet. Bedrooms have box-sprung divans and are warm and cosy, most welcome if visiting early in the season as the nights then turn cool.

These comforts, plus fine food cooked on kitchen boats moored alongside the main houseboat, and the ever-willing servants, make staying on a houseboat a time of pleasant aspects and much pampering. It is as pleasant to sit in of an evening as it is breathtaking to lounge on the flat canopied roof-top of the houseboat in the daytime admiring the grand scenery.

Attached to each houseboat is a *shikara*, a low row-boat in which, under chintzy awnings are soft cushioned seats. This boat takes one from the moored houseboat to the mainland or around the lake on trips. It is yours to command and is included with the rent. It will be paddled by a sturdy Kashmiri boy, seemingly always cheerful and helpful despite his long hours of duty.

To rent a houseboat one should call at the Tourist Office near the bus stand in Srinagar and arrange for a *shikara* to take you around to look at a selection before deciding on a particular one. As boat owners will let out unused houseboat bedrooms (just like a hotel), choose a small boat and it will be easy for you to arrange to have the whole boat for your party, especially if out of season.

Do not go to Kashmir if you are short of time. It is quite a journey getting there and to arrive and stay for less than, say, three days, is just not worth the effort.

If travelling by air the journey need not take long but the road/rail

24 Shikara boats on Lake Dal, Kashmir

journey can take two days. As Kashmir is a border territory, after baggage reclamation there is a military check and forms to be filled.

Under the British the whole region of Jammu and Kashmir was a princely State over which the ruler had complete control. (It was he who said that no foreigners could own land in Kashmir.) The State ticked over as a feudal country visited by wealthy Indians and by foreign visitors. Between the wars, and largely as a result of reading accounts of Kashmir and its glories, the amount of visitors increased and tourism was born. This resulted in more houseboats being built, more facilities for the tourists and a greater revenue for the State.

At Independence, the then ruler of Kashmir, Sheik Abdulla, had to decide whether to become a part of Pakistan, or to continue as a part of India. Despite the population's Muslim majority, which, it might have been expected, would have swayed Sheik Abdulla in favour of joining Pakistan, he nevertheless opted to stay within India. He left his decision rather late for, in fact, Pakistan was already crossing his borders and this intrusion caused the first Indo-Pakistan conflict.

Kashmir is, therefore, a very sensitive area, not only because of its proximity to Pakistan, but because eastwards lies China, which, in 1962 invaded the Ladakh area and caused India to be on its guard at all its northern borders, hence the form-filling by which all visitors register with the authorities.

No time seems long enough to visit the numerous sights around Kashmir. A month would be ideal, as then pony-trekking could be a part of the experience and one could go up into the mountains to Sonamarg and the Sind Valley where there are meadows of crocus and blue gentian, ice floes, and glaciers leading to snow-clad ranges.

To describe all the places around the Vale of Kashmir would need a book itself, of which there are plenty available. It is useful, though, to mention one or two places that might be missed, yet can be enjoyed even by the hasty traveller.

Go to Gulmarg, where there is the highest golf course in the world and where there is winter skiing and an outer circular walk running 11 km (7 miles) from which there are continuous excellent views of the Vale below and of the mountains – Nanga Parbat being one of them. At Gulmarg there are ancient Swiss-style bungalows and the Raj hotel, the Highland Park, which serves good tea and has beautiful gardens.

From Srinagar take a taxi or walk up to the top of Shankaracharaya Hill, from where the view of Lake Dal is superb. Visit the Shalimar Gardens and the other, less famous, Nishat Bagh. Take a boat from Srinagar and be paddled across Lake Dal, into Nagin Lake, altogether quieter, and from there go to Hazratbal, where there is the mosque in which is kept a hair of the Prophet Mohammed. Land here and walk around the narrow streets and see the higgledy-piggledy life of the people there. The setting is as idyllic as is the journey to get there. Half a day should be allowed, starting very early in the morning, so that you will also see the floating vegetable market, a conglomeration of boats in the middle of one of the backwaters containing vegetables among which will be seen exotics such as kohlrabi and lotus roots. Lotus roots are a delicacy and you should have your cook prepare them for dinner one evening.

Experience an evening on a *doonga*, a long pleasure boat, and recline against comfortable cushions and listen to Kashmiri ghazals, love songs

25 The highest golf course in the world, at Gulmarg in Kashmir

26 The Shalimar Gardens

sung to the accompaniment of the *rabab*, a type of violin, and the thrumming of earthenware pots known as *matkas*. If you are brave and hungry afterwards, go and have a 35 course Kashmiri meal called a Wazwan. The basic pilaf rice is served with 35 courses of lamb! The list seems endless: meat balls stuffed with paté, grilled spare ribs, etc. Take your time eating and don't drink beer. Take only small portions of each of the dishes and you will certainly eat your fill and have had a memorable culinary experience!

A word should be said about the water-traders who ply to and fro, pestering in what many have described as an intimidating manner. It is sufficient to instruct the owner of the houseboat, the man to whom you pay the rent, that under no circumstances do you wish traders to visit your boat, and you will experience little trouble. On the waters of the lake in your *shikara* your paddle-boy will keep traders at bay and he will do it better than you, in the language they understand.

Special fishing tours are now arranged. One company has the exclusive fishing rights on certain waters and offers a package holiday, by jeep or by car, from Srinagar. Included is tented accommodation. The cost also includes transportation from and back to Srinagar and between beats, the camp site, the services of guides, rods, fees and soft drinks and accommodation (see details under Tourist Agencies).

Punjab

The Punjab is one of the most prosperous parts of India. Divided into two parts in 1947, its capital, Lahore, became a part of Pakistan and a new capital was subsequently built, called Chandigarh.

In 1966 the State was again reorganized and from this was created the predominantly Hindi speaking State of Harayana, leaving the present Punjab largely Punjabi speaking and largely inhabited by Sikhs, who are now numerically in the majority.

The name Punjab means 'The Land of Five Rivers', though only two actually flow through present-day Punjab: the Sutlej and the Beas. It is the harnessing of these two waterways, combined with the constant hard work of all Punjabis, that has been responsible for the State being called the granary of India.

Scattered villages punctuate rolling countryside where farms and townships break up horizon after horizon of cultivated fields. It is a terrain which most travellers fly over, hastening either to Amritsar or to Chandigarh. Amritsar can be visited either direct from Delhi or Bombay or it can be a stop-over en route to or from Kashmir.

If one arrives around tea-time an overnight stop is sufficient time for seeing the main sight of interest – the Golden Temple. The most beautiful times to walk around the compound of the temple are at sunset or dawn.

When in Amritsar, and if time permits, a visit can be made to Jallianwala Bagh, scene of the famous massacre shown to such horrifying effect in the film 'Gandhi', and now a park. In the walls can still be seen bullet marks and one can also see the well into which people jumped in order to escape the bullets of the troops under the command of Brigadier-General Dyer.

In the old city, in the centre of an artificial lake similar to that surrounding the Golden Temple, there is a Hindu temple dedicated to Laxshmi and Narayan.

A short excursion easily undertaken by rickshaw is to the Fort of Govindgarh. This was built by Ranjit Singh, who was also responsible for gilding the Golden Temple with an overlay of copper which in turn was covered with gold leaf.

The city of Chandigarh is a show-place of the Punjabis. Planned by a group of renowned architects led and inspired by the Frenchman Le Corbusier, Chandigarh is a pre-stressed concrete combination of East and West. The city is built on the grid system and seems somewhat to lack soul. It is dusty and windy and antiseptic in feeling compared to the turmoil and exuberance of any of the old capitals of Indian States.

Haryana

If travelling by road to many of the interesting centres in northern India, then you will almost certainly have to pass through the State of Haryana. From Delhi to either Jaipur or Amritsar, to Kashmir or to Simla, Agra or even the Bharatpur Bird Sanctuary, the way is some distance through Haryana. The Haryanwis have taken advantage of their position and built a series of holiday service centres where one can rest awhile, get some petrol or spend a night in comfortable surroundings.

The State shares Chandigarh as a capital and, apart from Hindi, the people speak Haryanwi, a dialect of Hindi, and some Punjabi.

For Indian families going on a motoring holiday or on a holiday by bus this State has provided centres for complete family enjoyment, and by passing one to another the beauties of the State may be seen. For the busy and time-conscious foreign visitor, though, the State has little to offer other than an abundance of hospitality. If possible, visit the Pinjore Gardens at Kalka, a small town in the north of the State. From here there is the narrow-gauge railway that runs up to Simla. It is a delightful ride and a novel way of reaching one of India's most famous hill stations.

Himachal Pradesh

This State, formed when the Punjab was divided a second time, in 1966, is situated almost entirely in the foothills of the Himalayas.

There are three different areas: the bustling hill station of Simla with its restaurants and hotels and Western music, its flower shows and its historical reminders of the Raj; the whole valley of Kulu, through which runs the Beas river and where all around are incredible views of the high mountain peaks of the Himalayas, and finally the pilgrimage place called Dharamsala.

Simla is much the same now as it was in Kipling's time. The town is built across a crescent-shaped ridge, at an altitude of around 212 m (700 ft). 'Tiny red-roofed chalets, castle-like offices and a tin-topped bazaar are set among giant pines which add fragrance to the crisp Himalayan air', says the tourist handout and it is an apt description.

All along the ridge runs the main thoroughfare, called the Mall, where once the British banned all vehicles, and surrounding this are numerous walks. One can go to the Glen, to Summer Hill, Chadwick Falls, Prospect Hill and to the interesting Wildflower Hall, site of the former residence of Lord Kitchener. A new building has replaced the Kitchener one.

For railway enthusiasts there is the narrow-gauge railway running up from Kalka. It was built in 1903. On this line can be visited the Moghul Gardens of Pinjore, or Chali, the summer capital of the Maharaja of Patiala. Chali is enchanting and is worth a stop-over. The palace will accommodate you, or, if not, there are any number of hotels. Chali is 2250 m (7400 ft) high, has spectacular views and boasts the highest cricket pitch in the world!

There are so many places within a day's distance of Simla that time should be allowed to do justice to a visit. All days will not be fair-weather ones and warm clothing and umbrellas are advisable.

Kulu

The valley of Kulu and all roads from and to it are a walker's paradise, a trekker's dreamland and a way to fine mountain scrambles and climbs. One needs good footwear and good lungs! Pine and cedar clothe the mountain sides, interspersed with green pastures over which tower snow-capped peaks; it is an alpine region. The river Beas is well stocked with trout and can provide splendid fishing.

Never more than 1.6 km (1 mile) wide, the valley is 80 km (50 miles) in length, the whole of which is spectacular. In summer-time, from May to October, there is fruit in abundance: cherries, apricots, plums, apples and

27 At the snow-line in the foothills of the Himalayas

pears being cultivated in great quantity and sent off to the markets in India's cities from where much is exported, especially to the Gulf States.

Giant scarlet rhododendrons grow on the hillsides and the fields are full of flowers. In June the chestnuts bloom and, from then onwards, throughout the equable summer days, bees produce honey which is famous throughout the region.

Manali

The town of Manali lies at the top end of the Kulu Valley. It is popular with a mixture of peoples. Tibetans are there and Gaddis, the nomadic herdsmen who roam the upper hills. There is, too, a scattering of bungalows which belong to well-off Indians living down on the plain; they are summer residences, often left for months in the care of a watchman. There is a bazaar, some temples and many fantastic walks, but it is a long and primitive way to go for the average visitor to India.

Uttar Pradesh

Uttar Pradesh lies between the Punjab and Bihar on India's northern frontiers and is the most densely populated area of the country. The population is 111 million. In addition to those people whose home is in the State, there is a floating population of pilgrims which at any one time has been estimated at over 2 million.

The State is one of the most important religious and historical areas of India and offers, for the avid traveller, a unique experience of people, places and ideas.

The River Ganges rises in the north at Hardwar and runs the length of the State, to Bihar westwards, through West Bengal, to join the sea at Calcutta. On its way it passes the grand historical cities of Lucknow, Kanpur (Cawnpore) and Allahabad, eventually reaching Benares, now called Varanasi.

Delhi

The city of Delhi is one of the Union States in India. It was created as a province in 1912, formerly being a part of the Punjab. Its area was extended in 1915 by the incorporation of a part of what were then called the United Provinces, now Uttar Pradesh. It has an area of 1486 sq. km

(574 sq. miles) and a population of over 6 million. It is the capital of India and the city is vast.

It is called New Delhi to distinguish between what was the ancient city of Delhi and the new, commercial, political and residential area laid out to plans made by Sir Edward Lutyens. New Delhi is the third largest city in India and the main language is Hindi. The older parts contain the main bazaars, mosques and temples, and New Delhi is a spacious area with wide tree-lined streets and beautiful houses set beyond driveways and gardens. Here are the embassies and consulates and also the seat of government, parliament buildings and the official residence of the President of India, the Rastrapati Bhavan, whose gardens have recently been opened to the public.

In the old part of the city is the Red Fort. Built by Shah Jehan between 1639 and 1648, its red walls and towers and cupolas tend to dominate the old town. The quarters around it are a mish-mash of street traders and pavement dwellers. There is a son et lumiere show each evening at the Red Fort, which creates scenes of past historical events, both Indian and of the time of the Raj, ending with Independence. On the other side of the road from the Red Fort is the Jami Masjid, the great mosque of Old Delhi, reputed to be the largest in India. The mosque was built between the years 1644 and 1658 and has the customary four minarets, one of which can be climbed up for fine views of the city.

From the fort and past the mosque runs the Chandni Chowk, street of silversmiths and goldsmiths and jewellers and perfume sellers, which was once renowned for being the richest street in the world. As interesting as the congested street itself are the hundreds of small alleyways which lead off it and back on to it, where seemingly everything is sold.

Connaught Circus is the central hub of New Delhi and is a bewildering place of ever-widening circles of high colonnaded buildings which all seem the same. In the centre, if one can get to it through the dense traffic, is a park area of quite considerable size, emphasizing Lutyen's vision and scope.

A short walk away, but often missed by those who rush through Delhi, is the Jantar Mantar, the Maharajah Jai Singh's observatory. It is similar to the one at Jaipur but built of sandstone and marble. It is a pretty and a quiet place with lily pools and strange pink-coloured structures. There is one place in the outer wall where, as the sun rises, its beams pierce through a hole onto one of the structures. Ask one of the youths lolling around on the grass exactly where the hole is and he will show you, and also tell you what the beam of sunlight meant to the ancient astronomers.

The city coach tour will go to all the noteworthy places of Old and New Delhi and will also go to the outskirts, such as Humayan's Tomb and the Qutab Minar.

Hardwar

Situated at the foot of the Sawalik Hills, Hardwar sees the beginnings of

28 The Moti Masjid (Pearl Mosque) inside the Red Fort, Delhi

29 Jantar Mantar, Delhi, one of Jai Singh's observatories

30 Humayan's Tomb, Delhi

the River Ganges. It is, consequently, a very holy place. The waters here are frightfully cold and immersion is only for the brave, the healthy or the young though there are many ancient-looking Hindus to be seen quivering in the freezing water, water which is reputed to wash away all sins. The water rushes through an ever-widening gorge between high hills, with glimpses of distant snow-clad mountain peaks. The weather at Hardwar does become summer-mild, but at a time when European visitors to India are discouraged, in May to October; then all the northern region of Uttar Pradesh is radiantly beautiful.

Rishikesh

Here ashrams and gurus, sadhus and temples are to be found, and, inevitably, hippies. It was to Rishikesh that the Beatles went to be with the Guru Maharishi Mahesh Yogi and, for as long as the legend of the

Beatles lasts, so will their followers visit this hill region. The Maharishi runs a Transcendental Meditation Centre here and there is also the Divine Life Society, founded by Swami Shivanand. Round about the walks are beautiful and the scenery very grand.

Almora

If you have a car, or better still a jeep, then carry on to Almora. It is a picturesque hill station which was once a part of Nepal. It is infinitely beautiful, surrounded by a circle of hills, each with a temple on top.

Naini Tal

Another place nearby this region is Naini Tal – arguably the most attractive. Situated at an altitude of 1935 m (6350 ft), around a lovely lake, it was once the summer headquarters of the Government of Uttar Pradesh. It is now a popular resort with Indians. There is yachting, boating and fishing, chilly swimming and numerous walks to places with quaint names like China Peak, Marya Kanta and Tiffin Top.

Dehra Dun

Dehra Dun was (and still is for a few) a favourite place for the British. There is a public school – the Doon School – and many private schools, and there is the Indian Military Academy and the Indian Forest Research Institute. There is nothing much to do at Dun, but it is a good place from which to visit the hill station called Mussoorie, 22 km (13 miles) away up in the foothills of the Himalayas.

Mussoorie

Perched on a ridge of the Sawalik Hills above Dehra Dun, Mussoorie can easily be reached by local bus or by taxi. Once one has left the plain and started to climb, the journey becomes more and more spectacular.

On arrival, there being no vehicular traffic allowed on the main thoroughfares, your bags will be carried on the backs of porters – Gharawalis – the name of the local hill people.

Mussoorie is best visited, say for a week, between May and October. There are numerous hotels, incredible walks and Happy Valley, the Tibetan refugee township run by Mrs Chazotsang, niece of the Dalai Lama.

Agra

The Golden Age of Agra began with the Emperor Shah Jehan. He initiated the most splendid period of building in Agra, almost completely rebuilding the city. Shah Jehan was enthroned in 1626 and, during his reign, built the Jami Masjid, most of the palace buildings inside the Red Fort and, of course, the Taj Mahal. He also built the Red Fort and the Jami Masjid in Delhi and there is often confusion when looking back on photographs taken of both mosques and forts as to which is which.

Shah Jehan was eventually overthrown by one of his sons, Aurangzeb, who had treacherously killed two of his own brothers so as to secure the throne for himself. On entering the city of Agra, in 1658, he imprisoned his father, Shah Jehan, in the Red Fort, where he spent the last years of his life gazing across the river Jumna at the tomb of his second, much beloved, wife, Mumtaz – the Taj Mahal.

Much later Agra fell to raiding Jats, who in turn fell to the Marathas. The British took control only in 1803 and, apart from fighting at the time of the Indian Mutiny in 1857, Agra has remained a peaceful place and is very pleasant to visit.

The construction of the Taj Mahal commenced in 1632 and took, so it is said, 20,000 builders and craftsmen 22 years to complete. Shah Jehan had skilled craftsmen brought from all over the world to work on the tomb and one wonders not only at the result, but at the cause. It must have been a very great passion that caused so singular and costly and inimitable a monument to be built in memory of a woman. Mumtaz certainly is the only woman in history to have such an extravagant testimony of a man's love for her. She bore 14 children in 17 years and died whilst away with Shah Jehan on one of his battles. After being buried temporarily, her body was brought back to Agra and eventually laid to rest in the Taj Mahal.

The Taj Mahal is built of brick, clad in white marble both inside and outside and inlaid with semi-precious stones. It has panels of meltingly beautiful relief carvings of lotus blossoms and jasmine, the heads of the flowers purposefully carved drooping, as though in reverence. The main structure is flanked by identical minarets that rise 39 m (130 ft) high and are built slightly off true, leaning outwards to prevent damage to the tomb should they ever collapse. The main gateway is a huge structure itself and has on top of it 22 small domes, often called honey-pot domes, and the number is supposed to represent the time in years taken to complete the building of the Taj Mahal. The precious inlay work is so fine that no joints between the pieces can be seen, even through a magnifying glass – the jasper, agate, lapis lazuli, cornelian and bloodstone merge so perfectly with the surrounding marble that no join is discernible by either sight or touch. To give an idea of the skill needed for the result, one flower, measuring only 2.5 cm (1 in) square, consists of 60 different inlays. It is said that to build another Taj Mahal would cost £100,000,000.

I read a charming tale in a daily paper about a prosperous peasant who had just spent 100,000 rupees (£6,500) having built on the roof of his house a replica of the Taj Mahal out of love for his wife. She was quoted as saying that she thought it would make their lives more romantic!

The Taj Mahal was closed for the first time in 300 years in 1971 when India was at war with Pakistan. Then, because there was fear that Pakistani bombers would use the reflected light from the dome of the Taj as a guide, the whole of it was covered by a camouflage of straw matting intermixed with flowers and grass. There was no fear for the Taj itself, it being a Muslim shrine.

Fatehpur Sikri

Fatehpur Sikri is 40 km (25 miles) south-west from Agra and is an easy excursion to make, either by local buses or by taxi. Ideally one should contrive to spend a night there and witness the dawn rise in the utter silence of the ghostly place. It was built at the time of Queen Elizabeth I, when Shakespeare was writing his plays, and travellers of that time tell of its glory and opulence, of unheard of riches and of grandiose architecture, courtliness and fulsome living.

There was a mystic named Salim Chisti who was noted locally for his power to bless a supplicant so that a male child was (almost) guaranteed. The Moghul Emperor, Akbar, badly wanted a son and, on passing the village of Sikri, heard of the mystic and sought his blessing. This was in 1568. Soon afterwards Akbar's wife bore him a son. This event may or may not have been chance but for Akbar it was enough to confirm the mystic's power and for him to raise a city overlooking the village of Sikri.

Astonishingly the city took only 6 years to complete. It was finished in 1575. Palaces, courtyards, a fort and mosque and an artificial lake (since drained) were built. There was, and still is, an open-air chess board made of marble squares upon which ladies of Akbar's harem sat as chess pieces in a game and moved when ordered. The buildings are of red sandstone inlaid with marble. There is a white marble mausoleum built to house the remains of Salim Chisti. It is a confection of pierced marble screens and white domes. For a rupee you can tie a piece of coloured wool around one of the piercings and this will ensure that one day you will return.

Fatehpur Sikri was deserted after only 14 years. One would have thought that, although history has recorded with accuracy its wonders and life and times, time itself would have eroded the structures and India's heat would have cracked the courtyards and caused tracery balconies to collapse. This is not so: the city is as near perfect as when built and can be seen just as the populace left it. It is said that the local people living nearby nowadays keep away at night, fearing ghosts and wild beasts.

The countryside around undulates with small hillocks rising out of jungle scrub, crested with flame of the forest trees. From the top of the Panch Mahal, so called because of its five (panch) storied structure, there is a haunting view of the deserted city and country.

At the south end of the mosque is the great gateway called the Buland Darwarza. It is 40 m (134 ft) high, giving enough clearance for the tallest of elephants surmounted with the largest howdah. By the gateway is an incredible deep well above which rise the minarets of the mosque and its surrounding wall. From this wall local divers perform hair-raising leaps into the well below.

One should try not to miss an ornamental curiosity at Fatehpur Sikri called the Hiram Minar. Hiram means deer and a Minar is a tower. The building is a shooting tower from which Akbar used to pot at deer and antelope, driven towards it by beaters. Tradition has it that the tower stands over the grave of Akbar's favourite elephant. It is built of red sandstone and the unusual feature of it is that the outside of the round tower is studded from top to bottom with elephant tusks carved out of stone protruding from stars of inlaid marble.

On leaving Fatehpur Sikri, Akbar went first to Lahore and, after 15 years, in 1599, moved his court to Agra where he died in 1605. His son, the result of the miracle supposedly wrought by Salim Chisti, and the reason Fatehpur Sikri was built, was named Jehangir and he fathered Shah Jehan, builder of the Taj Mahal.

Lucknow

Lucknow is the capital of Uttar Pradesh, but for all this and its historic associations there are few foreigners who visit here. The Nawabs of Oudh ruled from Lucknow and kept control of north-central India for over 100 years after the end of the Moghul empire. Today, Lucknow is the principal city of the Shi'ite Muslims; other places in India like Agra and Delhi being strongholds of the Sunnite Muslims. The last Nawab was deposed and supported by the British, in 1856, one year before the events of the Indian Mutiny. The Residency stands today as it was over 100 years ago when it was under siege for 87 days. A daily son et lumiere presentation re-enacts the story of the mutiny.

Like Allahabad, Lucknow is very rewarding to stop and see. India is often regarded as a purely Hindu country, and experiencing some of the Muslim areas will give a more balanced perspective to the country as a whole.

Allahabad

This is a big sprawling city situated in a fertile part of Uttar Pradesh where the Jumna and the Ganges meet. The name Allahabad, City of God, was given by Akbar who created the city in 1583/4 and thenceforward used it as a provincial headquarters.

From the banks of the Jumna river, hard by the fort, one can see in the distance the place where the rivers meet. It is called the *Sangam*. The River Jumna is a bluish colour, the Ganges a muddy red and at the confluence they obliterate any sign of the lesser river which mingles its waters with them – the Saraswati.

The *Sangam* is a place of veneration and great pilgrimage. A Mela, or fair, is held on January 14th each year when nearly one million people come from all over India to bathe at the confluence of the two great rivers. The famous Kumbh Mela occurs once every twelve years. Then there are upwards of five million pilgrims crowding Allahabad. For a fine description of the Kumbh Mela, read Ved Mehta's *Portrait of India*. At any time of the year one can hire a boat to take one to the confluence. There you will see gruesome sights of dead bodies of suicides or accidental drownings, carcases waiting for a fortuitous current to swirl them under the water to oblivion.

Above the river scene of boats and beggars and pilgrims once rose

Akbar's Fort. There are still remains there today but they bear little resemblance to Akbar's vision. The British turned the fort area into a tropical Sandhurst, stripping off cupolas and balustrades and other decorations and leaving only an ugly, square, unremarkable mass.

The Undying Banyan Tree of Allahabad should be seen as much for its situation as for itself. It is in the Patel Puri temple which, consequent on the building of Akbar's Fort, is now underground; the fort being built on top of it. It has an entrance from a charming courtyard, redolent of a Daniels engraving. Grey-black buildings edge the open space, stone seats stand under a central tree and olive-coloured trees pierce the spaces between crumbling houses. Through a stone gateway there is a long sloping staircase of slippery steps leading to a subterranean gallery which runs around a central hall. There are niches around the walls containing idols, of which several represent Ganesh. At the four points of the compass there are lingams in niches. Lighting is by candles, which flicker as the devout pass by.

At the far end of the hall, glowing in unexpected daylight, is the Undying Banyan Tree. It is easy to be sceptical about its longevity, but one has to record that the Chinese traveller Huien Tsang mentions seeing it in AD 640. If it has been kept 'alive' since then it certainly deserves to be called undying. Whatever the truth of the miracle, its temple is set amidst timeless and unchanging surroundings.

Benares

Benares has to absorb a great deal of Hindu India: it is a premier place of pilgrimage. All Hindus hope to visit Benares within their lifetime and, whenever one is there, it is as though they were all visiting it at that moment, so crowded is the city. Hindus believe that to bathe in the waters of the Ganges at Benares, as the sun surges up into the sky, is a sure way of preparing for the next life. If only one member of a family can make the pilgrimage he will return to his town or village with prayers and with a vessel of Ganges water. Secondhand blessings are better than no blessing at all.

In the seventh century AD Benares was named Kasi, roughly meaning 'resplendent with divine light'. The city has always been the religious capital of Hindusim. Almost contemporary with Babylon or Nineveh, Benares is thought to be the oldest living city in the world.

Another, perhaps more appropriate, epithet might be 'city of death', for Benares is a city to which people come to die. Many are the hands that take their share of a man's fortune to reduce him (or her) to ash and to float him upon the sacred water of the Ganges. The rites of dying and of being disposed of can be a costly affair, including the cost of the funeral pyre, the priests and the burners, and put a family into debt for a very long time.

The purity of the water of the Ganges is legendary. Everything conceivable is thrown or flushed into the river long before it reaches

31 Hindu women bathing in the Ganges at Benares

Benares. The river is a depository for refuse for over 965 km (600 miles) from where it rises beyond Hardwar, under Mount Kailas, yet in spite of this pollution the water has a purity that is almost magical. Locals and pilgrims drink it. Some say the water is highly sulphurous and this purifies it, others that it has a high potash content, which could be true remembering the constant addition of human and wood ash. Whatever the reason and no matter its colour, it would seem to harm no one.

Dawn is the ideal time to hire a boat and float along the ghats (steps) viewing temples and palaces and bathing places. The chief cremation ghat is called Manikarnika and there can be seen the suttee stones of women who cast themselves onto their husbands' funeral pyre – a ritual now ruled illegal, but still practised, particularly in rural areas. Nearby is the Charanpadurka Shrine where one can see the footprints of Lord Shiva preserved, and the Shiva Temple.

32 The morning sun shines through the back streets of old Benares; the man carries household pots used for storing grain

Benares is baffling with its multitude of gods and statues and temples, with its garishness and civic uncleanliness. The dead journey to the fire, the ill and lame wait for death and all around is a pulsating life-force, surviving among the desperately over-crowded streets. Temples smoke and priests chant. Hippies slouch around, misty-eyed, chewing snacks and scratching at bites on bare legs. Everywhere money is being made, by beggar and by businessman.

I have referred to Benares as Benares, not as it is now called, Varanasi. In so unchanging a place, the change of name seems an affront to history. It certainly was a needless nationalistic gesture.

Nine kilometres (6 miles) away one can visit Sarnath where the Lord Buddha preached his first sermon.

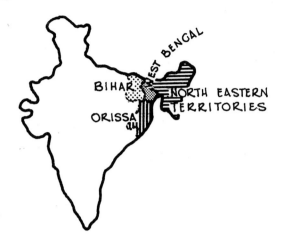

West Bengal

West Bengal is beset by political wranglings and by an immense refugee problem, two factors which inhibit progress and well-being yet which, with his characteristic cheerful optimism, the Bengali overcomes.

Eastern India is rich in iron ore, mica and coal, to say nothing about the great jute industry and the tea estates of Darjeeling and Assam. This whole area has been referred to as 'the Rhineland of India', an apt description as there is so much industrial river traffic running southward on the river Hoogly, eventually through Calcutta.

Calcutta

In the seventeenth century Calcutta was only a village. Today it is one of the largest cities in the world and is the capital of West Bengal. Besides this it is the largest city in India with a population exceeding eight million. The language is Bengali and Hindi, and Calcutta is the commercial hub of East India.

In its centre is an extensive park known as the Maidan. At the southern end stands Fort William, or what is left of it. To walk from this point back along Strand Road South is quite a distance but the walk will show aspects of town and river life which in some cases will be shockingly squalid. The famous Dalhousie Square is an example: once the pride of the business quarter, it has degenerated into a retreat for itinerant workers and their families who, having nowhere else, use the tank around which the square is built as a lavatory.

East of the Maidan is the area known as Chowringhee. This is the area of the main hotels, shops and eating places – the smarter end of Calcutta.

All around on the greenswards of the Maidan there are cattle grazing and men performing yoga exercises. There is football and cricket and

33 Howrah Bridge spanning the Hoogly River

tennis and people strolling. Both cattle and men use the whole area as a lavatory, so beware!

At the district called Alipore is the Belvedere, once the country house of Warren Hastings and now the National Library. The Botanical Gardens, a good excuse for crossing the River Hoogly, were founded in 1786 and contain, among a bewilderment of specimens attractively cared for, a 200 year old banyan tree, claimed to be the largest in the world. It covers an area of ground 304 m (1000 ft) in circumference. To reach there, take a boat from the Chandpal Ghat; the water of the river is khaki-coloured and the banks a mass of oleaginous mud, but the views are good.

For church, temple and mosque seekers there is St John's Church, Calcutta's oldest place of Christian worship, where Job Charnock, founder of Calcutta, is buried. Job Charnock was the organizer of the first merchant traders and started a settlement for them at Kalikata (1689) from which the present Calcutta derives its name. He was a resolute and religious man, so much so that he rescued a woman from the funeral pyre of her husband and subsequently married her. He deserves a rather better memorial than that in the gloomy, unkempt churchyard of St John's. There is also the Nakhoda Mosque, the Kalighat Temple and the Swami Vivekananda Temple of Dakshineswar.

The city is sprawling, confusing and exhausting and all rather seedy, earning it its rather apt description of 'the disembowled city'. The days of gracious living, of coaches and horses, of summer night balls, tennis parties and badminton matches have vanished. Calcutta has ceased to be 'the invention of the British' and is daily succumbing to a political and civic lack of care which, if not halted, will certainly isolate Calcutta from all but the most ardent visitors' itinerary.

Away from Calcutta, West Bengal is very different: lush and hospitable, imbued with the Bengali's gracefulness and artistry, manifest through ancient customs and everyday living.

34 Nakhoda Mosque, Calcutta

35 The business heart of Calcutta; the domed building is the General Post Office near Dalhousie Square

36 Central Chowringhee, part of the Maidan and downtown Calcutta

At 354 km (220 miles) to the north of Calcutta is the home of the Sultan Suraj-ud-Daula, responsible for the 'Black Hole' incident. This is the attractive town called Murshidabad. It is a typical Bengali town, with a distinctive feature being an 'Italianate' palace called the Nizamat Kila. Here glass chandeliers dangle in the breezes in contrast to the marble cartouches atop noble pillars which are covered in bird lime. The palace stands by a river which one has to cross to see the tomb of Suraj-ud-Daula and the Pearl Lake. Not many tourists go there but it is possible to stop off when en route from Calcutta to Darjeeling.

Darjeeling
If you travel to Darjeeling by air from Calcutta and do not stay there for more than fifteen days, then all the formalities that will be necessary will be the endorsement of your passport on arrival at Badogra. Darjeeling is referred to by the Indian Government as a 'sensitive area' and if, therefore, you choose not to go by air but brave the long (but fascinating) bus journey, or to go by train, then before you leave you will have to obtain a permit. Permits can be obtained either before actually leaving for India, by applying to any Indian Embassy, High Commission or Consulate, or from tourist agencies in Calcutta or the Foreigners Registration Office at 237 Acharya Jagdish Bose Road, Calcutta – not far from the Victoria Memorial.

Darjeeling has breathtaking views over the Kanchenjunga Ranges of the Himalayas. April, May and June are some of the best times for visiting, and also between late September and early October. A long-sleeved cardigan would be needed at times, and an umbrella will come in handy, but these are readily available at local shops. You need good legs for walking around Darjeeling – it is a place of steep hills, of mountain pathways and flights of steps interconnecting and rambling around the

37 Darjeeling, where you need good legs to walk the numerous hillways

township in a delightful way. The town is over 2000 m (7000 ft) high and the air is rare. Another 300 m (100 ft) up is Tiger Hill from where can be seen magnificent views of Mount Everest and, if one is up early enough, quite glorious sunrises. Arrangements to visit Tiger Hill are made by most hotels.

There are also several tea gardens which welcome visitors and show the process of tea cultivation and harvesting. There is the first passenger ropeway to be constructed in India, where, if you wish to ride on it, it is better to check first that seats are available and that it is actually running.

If you did not go to Darjeeling by either bus or train then try to make enough time for a ride down on the toy-train to Jalpaiguri. Stay the night there and return the next day. The journey will be well worthwhile and, certainly for the railway enthusiasts, will make up for any disappointments at Darjeeling, the most frequent being *not* seeing the great mountain ranges because of cloud and mist.

Kalimpong

The journey to Kalimpong (50 km [31 miles] from Darjeeling) is arguably more interesting than Kalimpong itself, which is a quiet place and very Tibetan. It is, though, an ideal place from which to have a walking holiday. Set among the Deolo and Dirbindra hills at about 1200 m (4000 ft), there are fine views from the surrounding gently rolling hills. Nearby is Lopchu, which has given its name to a famous Darjeeling tea. The babies here sit around in groups, some in knitted hats and their small black eyes twinkle like moist currants in a plum duff. Their parents sit in the sun also, knitting garments which will eventually find their way onto the pavements of Delhi and other cities where these hill people sell their woollen wares during India's winter chill.

Siliguri

Siliguri is the biggest town in north Bengal and is rather brash and modern, with vulgar signs and much plastic to be seen in the bazaars. It is the main transit point for travelling up to Darjeeling, to Kalimpong and to the States of Assam, Sikkim and the Eastern Provinces. All around here are tea gardens and railways! Siliguri is one of the most important railway junctions in north-eastern India. The popular mountain toy-train passes through here, and there is also the long-distance bus station for those who prefer to travel by road. From here one can take a bus to Kathmandu in Nepal. There are also good trekking facilities.

Bihar

Unless one is a very determined traveller one tends to cross over the land of Bihar. Today it is one of the most backward places in India. It is a melting pot of undisciplined police and uncontrollable people. The State is frequently in the Indian newspapers either for atrocities such as bride burnings or the blinding of prisoners, and for smuggling, a lucrative occupation for many.

In past times this was the area of India from where the great King Asoka ruled his kingdom. Patna, the capital of Bihar, was then called Pataliputra. Peace and prosperity and religious tolerance reigned and at the Nalanda University studies included the philosophy of Buddhist thought. Now, university life in Bihar is restless and politically active and the city of Patna, sprawled along the Ganges in a similar fashion to Benares, is a place of intrigue and lawlessness. Money and power are the great corruptors of Bihar yet it would be less than fair to give the impression that these regressive sores are only prevalent in Bihar; all too sadly they exist elsewhere in India and the rest of the world.

Patna

There are some fascinating sights to be seen at Patna, and no harm will befall the tourist stopping there. Patna stretches 13 km (8 miles) along the Ganges and, starting from the Governor's Palace, at the 'British' end called Bankipore, one can walk through streets and on the embankment, through government buildings, the High Court and the huge Patna Museum. Here can be seen remains of the earlier civilization of Pataliputra. Eventually one comes to the enormous Golghar, really a granary in which to store against famine. This beehive-like structure is 27 m (90 ft) tall and 'might contain 137,000 tons' (Murray's *Handbook*). Steps to the top ascend around the outside of this amazing structure and once on top there is a fine view of the city and of the Ganges.

At Gulzaribagh, to the east of Patna, there is the site of the East India Company's opium factory and warehouse which today is a printing works. Opium was not only used for smoking and for producing hallucinations and mental escape, it was a powerful pain reliever, and one to which Robert Clive (of India) resorted. Firstly it was for the gout he suffered and later on in his life he took opium to relieve anxiety and fearful headaches caused by his attacks of depression. (Eventually he committed suicide by slitting his throat.)

Day tours can be made to Nalanda and to Rajgir, both Buddhist centres, and to Bodh Gaya, the 'Mecca' of Buddhism. It was here that Guatama sat beneath the bo tree and attained enlightenment. The sacred bo tree now seen growing is said to be a direct descendant of the original tree. There is a story that a sapling of the original tree was taken over to Sri Lanka by the Emperor Asoka's son, Mahindra, when he went there to spread Buddhism, and in turn a sapling of that was brought back to Bodh Gaya. Whatever the story it is sufficient that for 25 centuries man has considered this place holy and for thousands of years pilgrims from all over the world have come here to meditate, study, rest and learn.

North from Bodh Gaya, and often confused with it, is Gaya, sacred to the Hindus. Here the devout will make a round of all the holy places and then will offer *pindas*, funeral cakes, for the peace of all departed souls. The centre of a pilgrimage is the temple dedicated to Vishnupada in whose *sanctum sanctorium* is a footprint of Lord Vishnu, imprinted in solid rock. It is surrounded by a silver basin.

Near the temple is the Bramajuni Hill, up which are a thousand stone-cut steps. If you make the climb to the top you will have spectacular views of the surrounding country.

Orissa

Orissa lies along the north-eastern coastline of India, below Calcutta and the Hoogly and the Sunderbans, and meets Andhra Pradesh in the south near Bheranpore. The language spoken is Orya.

The State is predominantly rural and has fertile plains running down to the coast behind which rise the Eastern Ghats and the table-lands of the Central Plateau.

Thought of as either a tribal area or a seaside or holiday place, Orissa was left very much alone and undeveloped and it was not until after Independence that a cohesive State was formed out of the small Raja States that comprised most of the area.

Now this somewhat backward area has changed, and though Orissa maintains its quiet and distinct character, it is being developed, nevertheless – the Hirakud dam being a magnificent example. Some say that industrial infiltration into the hinterlands will spoil its character, after its way of tribal life and pollute its ancient societies, but it ever was thus when progress was thrust upon peoples.

Bhubaneswar

This is the capital of Orissa and is a town of temples. The town is dominated by the Great Lingaraj Temple, thought by many to be the first Hindu temple in India. It is set in a huge walled compound around which are set many small shrines. Its great tower rises 39 m (127 ft) in the middle of the compound and is divided into vertical sections, each of which is richly carved. This tower is hollow and one can climb to the top by an inner staircase. Lord Curzon, who was responsible for much of the preservation and restoration of the monuments of ancient India, built a platform near the northern wall of the temple. It is a viewing platform from where a visitor who is non-Hindu can see parts of the inner temple. It was Lord Curzon who organized the restoration of the Taj Mahal at Agra.

Konarak

To visit this area of India and not to go and see the Sun Temple at Konarak is like going to Rome and not seeing the Vatican.

The Sun Temple was built in the thirteenth century AD, in the shape of a huge chariot for the Sun God. The chariot has 24 enormous wheels and seven horses pulling it and stands 70 m (230 ft) high – on the sand. Konarak is on the shores of the Bay of Bengal and is a shore temple rivalling all others. Here, among the multiplicity of carvings, are many that are erotic, representing sexual union in explicit detail. If possible, they are finer than those at Khajuraho. Some of the figures are life-like and some tiny, as those on the spokes of the great stone wheels. The whole is reputed to have taken 1200 sculptors twelve years to complete; the wonder is that it did not take longer.

Puri

To reach Puri from Konarak one must return to Bhubaneswar and start again coastwards. At Puri one can bathe in the warm waters of the sea, surf over the rolling waves and watch the fishermen bring in their catch. At Puri is the Jagannath Temple.

38 The great Lingaraj Temple at Bhubaneswar, Orissa

This great shrine is dedicated to the Lord of the Universe. Here, unlike at Bhubaneswar, there is no caste or religious distinction and all are welcome to worship and pray. (We get the word juggernaut from Jagannath.)

In the month of June, before the rains and, oddly, when it is hottest, Lord Jagannath is taken out of his temple in an enormous temple car. It is 13 m (45 ft) high and 10 m (35 ft) square and is supported on 16 wooden wheels. It is pulled along the broad central avenue of Puri by thousands of eager, excited and often ecstatic pilgrims (see Festivals and Fairs).

The Jagannath Temple has more than 6000 male adults serving as priests, custodians or guides, some of whom can seem intimidating. In Orissa, and in particular in Puri, they are important people.

Chilka Lake

This lake is quite extensive, being 72 km (45 miles) long and in parts 16 km (10 miles) wide, and has as a background the hills of the rising Eastern Ghats. Here one can boat and fish, or just laze around. There is a comfortable tourist bungalow for those who wish to stay. A further 13 km (8 miles) along the coast is Gopalpur-on-Sea, where the swimming is excellent and from where excursions can be made into the surrounding

39 Lion bracket support with warrior, eleventh-century AD, Orissa

hills to see the sulphur springs at Taptapani and the life lived by the tribal, Adavasi, people who inhabit this region.

North Eastern Indian Territories and Sikkim

Assam is perhaps the best known State in this region but recent strife has inhibited travel there. There is no restriction to visiting this area and a quick and speedy way to go is, of course, by air. To do justice to making the journey there one should really plan a separate time in Assam. All arrangements for this can be made from Delhi or from Calcutta, or by writing to one of the travel agents mentioned at the end of this book.

Gauhati is the capital of Assam, where Assamese is the spoken language. From here tours of the region can be arranged to places such as the Kaziranga Game Reserve.

The names of other territories in this eastern region are Manipur, Meghalaya, Nagaland, Tripuram Arunachal Pradesh and Mizoram.

Rajasthan

Geographically Rajasthan has miles of desert border region common with Pakistan to the west; here the land spreads out into the Great Indian Desert, huge tracts of which are now being irrigated and inhabited. Southwards, the Aravalli range of hills divides Rajasthan into two large areas: the north-western and the south-eastern. It is the former that is largely desert, the latter having a varied terrain of hill and table-land farming.

Rajasthani people are distinctive in their dress. The men among the farm worker class will wear only a dhoti, a vest, and, on the head, a wide turban-like cover. Their womenfolk dress mainly in saris of plain colours of red, salmon, saffron and green. On market days, on ceremonial occasions, or at festivals, the men will wear tight fitting pajama-like trousers called *churidars*, a *kurta* and a small coat and, on their head, a *pugri*, or turban, wide enough to cover and shade their head and face, the cloth from which the *pugri* is wound being 16 m (54 ft) long.

Rajasthani women often dress in a skirt and half-sleeved bodice which leaves the midriff bare. They will also wear an *odhni*, a mantle which covers the head. Most married women cover their heads completely, it being considered immodest to show their face in public. Their skirts will have as much as 36 m (120 ft) of material and will be embroidered and have fancy beads sewn into them.

Jewellery, too, plays a great part in the appearance of the Rajasthani, and not only for adornment – it is a means of keeping and showing wealth. Rural or town women will wear heavy anklets of either silver or ivory, and ornate earrings and head ornaments. Men often have an earring looped through the lobe of one ear, and all women, rich or poor, wear glass bangles, ubiquitous ornaments throughout India.

The season to visit Rajasthan is between October and March. Be cautioned, though, as it can be disappointingly wet in southern Rajasthan well into November and it will be cold, especially at night, until mid-January. Blankets, hot-water bottles and fires will be the order of the night!

Jaipur

Jaipur is the capital city of Rajasthan. The city was planned and laid out by the Maharajah Sawai Jai Singh (1727), a Rajput warrior king who had great taste and a consuming interest in astronomy. Jai Singh once inhabited the fortress palace of Amber, 11 km (7 miles) outside Jaipur. When Moghul power in the area began to wane he decided to move his court to the nearby plain where there would be greater accessibility to water.

He must also have been encouraged by his reception in Delhi on paying his respects to Aurangzeb. Aurangzeb was not known for his docility, rather the opposite, in fact, as he had killed off most of the members of his family and imprisoned his father in the Red Fort at Agra in order that he would certainly 'inherit' ultimate Moghul power.

The story is told of how the Jaipur ruler, Jai Singh, went to Delhi and, as he was about to present the Emperor with gifts, Aurangzeb flew into a rage and shouted 'Your ancestors gave me much trouble and were disloyal to my family, say what you deserve of me before what you desire'. Jai Singh was thunderstruck and could not reply. Aurangzeb then grasped both the outstretched hands of the prince and continued 'Of what use are your arms now?'

'Your Imperial Majesty,' replied Jai Singh, 'during a wedding the bridegroom takes the bride's hand in one of his own and from then on he is bound to protect her for the rest of his life. Now that the Emperor of

India has taken my hands into his what have I to fear? With your Majesty's long arms to protect me what other arms do I need?'

Aurangzeb was so greatly impressed with the young ruler's reply that he drew him close and said 'You excel your ancestor in intelligence and ability. Indeed you are *Sawai* Jai Singh, let this be your title henceforth and also that of your successors' (Sawai means one and a quarter times).

Sawai Jai Singh's ambition was to make Jaipur one of the finest cities in India. Planned with the help of European architects, astronomers and mathematicians, the city rose in pink sandstone and white marble to a simplistic plan of six rectangular blocks set within a surrounding wall. The need for defence seemed a prudent safeguard against attack, if not from the Moghuls, then from nearby Marathas.

On walking round the 'Pink City' one wonders at the labour that would have been needed to build it and at the management of that labour. Were there whips and masters and punishments and non-payment of dues for both labour and for materials? There must have been an army of elephants and camels carrying supplies, and a milling mass of people, possibly trying to make sense out of chaos. The lavish use of space would have amazed many. The main roads are 33 m (110 ft) wide and all secondary ones 17 m (55 ft) wide. The crenellated wall was built 6 m (20 ft) high and 3 m (9 ft) thick and has eight gateways.

The city, now, seems all enchantment and light. The vision of Sawai Jai Singh was realized and has achieved the patina of time and become one of the most unusual sights in India.

The City Palace is in the centre of the city and is still the home of the Jaipur royal family. There are many notable structures inside the palace

40 The City Palace, Jaipur

grounds but perhaps the most captivating is the Mubarak Mahal, built of delicately carved marble and rising high against the blue sky.

In Jaipur there is the largest of the observatories built by Sawai Jai Singh; known as the Janta Mantar it is said to be the best preserved of these observatories.

The instruments were designed to measure such things as local time, the sun's delineation, azimuth and altitude and the position of fixed stars and planets, and to determine eclipses. It is difficult to understand how these surreal structures could have been conceived let alone how they were used.

Amber

Amber lies to the north-east of Jaipur 11 km (7 miles) on the road to Delhi. The palace and fort crown a rocky hill amidst the most beautiful surroundings. The name Amber comes from one of the titles of Lord

41 The Ganesh Pol, or Elephant Gate, at Amber Palace

42 Riding on elephant back up to Amber Palace

Shiva, Ambarisha, and was the capital of the Kachhawa Rajputs for nearly six centuries, until Sawai Jai Singh founded the present Jaipur.

The Amber Palace is an exquisite example of Rajput architecture. From below it looks magical, spread along a hill range and reflected in a large pool. You will be exhorted to go up by elephant and perhaps it is worth the experience, though by far the better way to ascend the hill is to walk, either up the way the elephants go or via a short-cut on the side of the hill.

Unfortunately group tours have to stick to schedule. There are, though, days of leisure and if you have one such when staying at Jaipur then spend the time at Amber.

Also visit Galta, a deep temple-filled gorge, and Gaitor, where the royal tombs are. Try not to miss the Jal Mahal water palace, set in the middle of a nearby lake and reached by a causeway.

If you hire a car for the day then you can also go up to the Tiger Fort, 6 km (4 miles) from Jaipur, and the Sisodia Rani Palace and gardens, 8 km (5 miles) off on the Agra Road. If you do book a car make sure that you arrange to start at dawn – you really have to be up with the sun and away. Arrange for the hotel to provide packed food – breakfast as well as lunch.

It cannot be mentioned too often that one should settle the cost of car hire before setting off and, at the end of the agreed time, pay only the arranged amount. Remember, though, that the driver will only be employed by others (unless you actually know that he owns the car) and if he has helped you well, then a tip for him of ten per cent of the total is only just.

Ajmer

At 132 km (82 miles) to the south-east of Jaipur lies Ajmer in a beautiful valley surrounded by hills. The town derives its name from 'the invincible hill' called Ajayameru. Akbar annexed the area to the Moghul empire in 1556 and, because of its strategic importance, made it his military headquarters.

It was at Ajmer that Sir Thomas Roe, Ambassador of King James I of England, presented his credentials to the Emperor Jehangir, son of Akbar, in 1616. Later the eldest son of Shah Jehan was born at Ajmer and the war of accession among the sons of Shah Jehan was fought at the battle of Dorai, near Ajmer, in 1659. Shah Jehan built the graceful pavilions on the embankment of the Ansagar Lake, around which the town is built. This lake was constructed between 1135 and 1150. It is related that the king of that time, Anaji, killed so many of his enemies at this spot that in order to wash away the sight of so much bloodshed he had it filled with water by damming a river. The long elegant embankment, with its five marble pavilions and gardens, called the Daulat Bagh, contributes not a little to the calm of this beautiful place.

Udaipur

Udaipur is a dazzling place of white buildings, lakes and low distant hills. Water assumes a tremendous importance throughout India but it takes on miraculous overtones when it is situated in an arid region, as are the lakes at Udaipur. Ancient temples, luxurious gardens and marble palaces make the lakeside city of Udaipur uniquely enchanting. In 1921 the then Prince of Wales remarked, 'There is nothing between Madras and the northern passes quite like Udaipur'.

The city, some 609 m (2000 ft) above sea level, was originally the capital of the State of Mewar and takes its name from the Maharana Udai Singh who founded it in the middle of the sixteenth century. The Maharanas of Udaipur are the highest-ranking Rajput rulers. The Maharana is known as 'the Sun King' and has the emblem of the sun on his standard, an emblem which can be seen all around the city and especially in the City Palace.

A wall encircles the city in which stand five gates studded with iron spikes, once a protection against battering rams. The main palace stands high over the waters of the principal lake, Lake Pichola. From this lake there is a canal which connects it to another, the Fatteh Sagar. En route one passes through the Swaroop Sagar, a smelly place and hardly a credit to the authorities.

43 Udaipur Palace: a pierced marble screen

Lake Pichola is bounded by wooded hills and has bathing ghats going down into its waters. In the middle of the lake is the Jag Nivas Palace, built by the Maharana Jagat Singh II in 1756 and extended by subsequent rulers. The granite and marble palace consists of a group of apartments with courts and fountains and gardens and is now the Lake Palace Hotel. Try and visit the other palace set out in the lake, the Jagmandir. This is built in sandstone and is set in tranquil gardens.

Just 3 km (2 miles) to the east of Udaipur are the ruins of the ancient city of Ahar, with the cenotaphs of the early rulers of Mewar; 9 km (6 miles) further on one comes to the lake called Udai, constructed by the Maharana Udai Singh and essential to the irrigation of surrounding land. Farther away but easily accessible by bus is the large lake called Rajsamund which has a masonry embankment entirely paved with marble. Cut into the stone of the embankment is the longest Sanskrit inscription in India; it recounts the history of the Mewars. Another 'largest' feature near Udaipur is Lake Jaisamund, one of the largest sheets of man-made water in the world. Built in the seventeenth century, it has six marble *chatris* around the embankment, each with a carved elephant in front and a shrine to Shiva inside. Islands in the lake are inhabited by the Bhil and Mina tribal people. Many of the Bhil people of Rajasthan travel all over India seeking temporary farm or road work. They wear colourful costumes of red cotton into which are sewn patterns of embroidery and small mirrors. They wear much silver jewellery.

Chittorgarh
Once the capital of the Sisodia Rajputs, Chittorgarh is the quintessence of Rajput pride and valour. It was here that the defeated Rajputs repeatedly gave up their lives rather than surrender. The men donned saffron robes and rode out of the great fort to their deaths, leaving their womenfolk and children to die by self-immolation on a great funeral pyre which they built themselves.

Today the fort is a vast ruin but there are still impressive reminders of its past glory, not the least of which is the Tower of Victory, erected by Rana Kumba to commemorate his victory over Mohammed Khilji of Malwa in 1440. The tower rises nine stories high and one can climb to the top and from there see the whole of the fort area and the distant country.

Jodhpur
After Jaipur, Jodhpur is the largest city in Rajasthan. It stands on the edge of the Thar Desert and is a harsh place of hot winds and stark fortified houses; towering over all is the Meherangarh Fort.

Jodhpur was founded in 1458 by Rao Jodha, the head of the Rathor clan of Rajputs. The old city is surrounded by a wall and contains a fascinating jumble of mainly white-painted houses with seemingly little room between for traffic, yet camels and donkeys lumber their way through. It is from here that the baggy horse-riding trousers, called jodhpurs, get their name.

44 The Tower of Victory at Chittorgarh

The main attraction of Jodhpur is undoubtedly the fort. Set up high on a rocky eminence, it dominates the city. It is scarped on every side, especially on the south side, where the huge palaces have been built as though a continuation of the perpendicular cliffs.

The principal buildings in the fort are the palaces, with their beautifully decorated and carved panels and their latticed windows of pierced sandstone. It is a photographer's paradise, but over-exposure is a danger because the light is absolutely blinding.

Jaisalmer

From Jodhpur one can get a train or bus to Jaisalmer. The train would be more comfortable and, arguably, more reliable but the bus will, eventually, get you there. The journey will take 10 hours. Best of all ways is the night sleeper train; this also takes 10 hours but you will arrive refreshed.

Though remote, Jaisalmer is gradually creeping into the tour itineraries. A stay of two nights is needed to do all the attractions justice. Recently the Indian Tourist Board started running a special train from Delhi which goes to Jaisalmer. 'The Palace on Wheels' as it is called, is described in the chapter on railways.

Jaisalmer is famous for embroidery, mirror-work, rugs and tie-dye materials. At various seasons of the year there are camel races, music festivals and there is son et lumiere. It is not a very sophisticated place and one must be prepared to experience rough life and rough conditions. It is a desert city, a place of camel-train trading and harsh conditions.

Bikaner

A desert town in the north of Rajasthan, Bikaner is in the Thar Desert, beyond waves of sand dunes, and was founded by Rao Bikaji in 1465. The city is surrounded by 8 km (5 miles) of fortified walls. As at Jodhpur, a massive fort dominates the city. Just outside the wall is the Lalgarh Palace, famed for its pierced screen work. Bikaner was once a staging post for the caravan routes and is noted for breeding excellent camels today.

Pushkar

Lake Pushkar is a place of pilgrimage for Hindus. The setting is peaceful except during the Pushkar Festival, or fair, held each year in October–November. At this time upwards of 200,000 people bring with them 50,000 cattle, horses and camels for dealing and racing and a general pilgrimage. There are dance programmes arranged by the Rajasthani State Tourist Board and the fair has become one of India's biggest and most colourful events.

Mount Abu

Just in Rajasthan, on the border with Gujarat, Mount Abu is a hill station and a pilgrimage place, mainly for the Jain sect; in fact, if it is not *the* most important Jain pilgrimage place then it must be one of the most

45 Ceiling carving of marble at the Dilwara Temple, Mount Abu

important. The famous Dilwara temples there are renowned throughout the world, not only for their sanctity but for their incredible carvings.

The interior of the Vimal Vashi temple has to be seen to be believed. From the outside the building is quite plain but the interior is richly carved in white marble, most of which has honeyed with time.

Kotah

Kotah lies on the eastern bank of the river Chambal, one of the great rivers of central India. The city of Kotah is enclosed by massive bastioned walls and has a fascinating museum and palace. In the museum, called the Saraswati Bhandar, there is a valuable collection of thousands of beautifully illustrated manuscripts pertaining to local affairs and to Rajput history. There are some public gardens and a lake with pavilions and delightful walks, all, alas, suffering from neglect.

Bundi

Bundi is 39 km (24 miles) west of Kotah, situated in a narrow gorge. The main street is stone paved and is set 1.8 m (6 ft) below the level of the main shops – it serves as an overflow for the Naval Sagar, a water tank at its western end.

Above the Naval Sagar, and quite a climb, is a mass of palace buildings. The palaces are approached by a steep ramp which leads through high gateways flanked by stone elephants.

Both Kotah and Bundi are difficult to reach because of train changes, and the change from broad gauge to metre gauge, but if one does make the effort a visit there is very rewarding.

Alwar

This is a curious place with a gory past, and a present which is anything but orderly. The tales about the Maharaja Sir Jai Singh are legion, from using human babies as bait when out tiger shooting, to being a homosexual 'who chose his officers with sensual care and forced them later'. His most infamous act was committed when playing polo at Mount Abu. Being dissatisfied with a pony's performance, he poured petrol over it and sent it up in flames. He was removed from power by the British in 1933 and died five years later in Paris.

Bharatpur

Though an interesting area, Bharatpur is mainly visited now for its bird sanctuary. It is an overnight stop from Delhi or a day trip from Agra. Since 1964 shooting has been banned. The actual sanctuary is situated 8 km (5 miles) outside Bharatpur, at a place called Keoladeo Ghana. In Bharatpur itself there is a fort and a palace which once belonged to the ruling family, the whole being very attractive.

Gujarat

In this western State of India the scenery varies from the bleak coastal regions of the Kutch, on the Arabian Sea, to the northern Aravali Hills which lead to Rajasthan. Over eastwards, towards the Western Ghats, are vast tracts of arable land producing the region's vegetables and fruit. Notable are the mango and the chikoo, the latter looking rather like a tennis ball and tasting like a cross between a fig and a pear. Southwards, along the Ghats, run fields of paddy and palm-fringed beaches until one reaches the borders of Maharastra, near Daman. Gujarati is the language spoken, with Hindi. Gujarat is a stronghold of the Jains, was the home of Mahatma Gandhi and is the last place in India where the lion still survives.

Ahmedabad

Ahmedabad stands on the river Sabamarti, which cuts a wide handsome swathe through the city, often referred to as the Manchester of India because of its many cotton mills.

The Jami Masjid, the great mosque in the centre of the old city, was built in 1423 by the city's founder, Sultan Ahmed Shah. This mosque is built on a grand scale and is cool and quiet inside. Another mosque, the Rani Sipri Mosque, has some of the very finest of sandstone carving to be seen in Gujarat. Also built of sandstone is the Sidi Sayyid Mosque, near

46 The Rani Sipri Mosque showing the delicately pierced carving

the Lal Darwaza, centre of modern Ahmedabad. Here are to be seen the world-famous windows of stone tracery, with superb examples of filigree carving.

Spending two or three days in this city, with its river and parks and bazaars, can be very pleasant, and local bus tours will take in such places as Kankaria Lake, the Shaking Minarets (don't go up if you suffer from vertigo) and the Sabamarti Ashram set up by Mahatma Gandhi in 1915 as a retreat and from where he began the salt march in 1930. See, too, the Jain Temple of Hathee Singh, a miracle of marble carving, completed in 1848, and try to go to the Dada Hari step well. An auto-rickshaw will take you there and the same transport could be used for a trip of 16 km (10 miles) to see the Sarkhej Rauza, an architectural complex of great beauty arranged around a stepped tank. Here there are no arches in the buildings, only pierced stone trellises and horizontal supports adding unusual elegance to mosque and palace. The floors of the palace, incidentally, are swept with peacock feather dusters!

47 The famous Shaking Minarets at Ahmedabad

Baroda

Unlike Ahmedabad, Baroda has a small dirty river running through it which, had civic history been different, could have been made into a feature as attractive as any of the smaller town rivers of Europe. As it is, the Vishwamitri River, when not in spate, is little more than a sewer; fortunately it is seldom seen, being hidden in a deep declevity.

Among places of interest in Baroda is the Lakshmi Vilas Palace. Although not generally open to the public, permission can be obtained (with forbearance) at the offices of the palace. Do not forget to ask permission to use a camera, or you will be stopped by the palace staff.

The University buildings are pleasant to stroll through and lead towards the Sayaji Bagh, the extensive public park of great beauty and the pride of the city. Here there is a museum and art gallery, a zoo and a miniature railway.

There is another museum at Baroda, the Fateh Singh Museum, which houses much of the Maharajah's private collection of furniture, porcelain and paintings. The museum building was once the school for the children of the royal family. Beyond and behind it is a private cricket ground and an alligator pen.

If spending more than a day or so in Baroda then go for a trip out to Champaner (47 km [29 miles]) – a good place for a picnic. There is a mosque, a temple, a lake, a hill-top temple and fort, and a good climb to the top – 448 m (1471 ft).

Jamnagar

A major city of the area called Saurashtra and the capital of that name, Jamnagar is known to all Indians as the home of Prince Ranji, the great cricketer. The city is built around a lake with an island in the middle that is reached by a bridge. On the island is the Lokhota Fort and museum housing a good collection of sculptures and artefacts from surrounding archaeological digs. On the island is a curious well in what was the old arsenal. The water in the well can be drawn up by blowing into a small hole in the floor. Go and try it!

Junagadh

Really worth visiting and easy of access from Bombay by air, Junagadh is situated at the foot of the holy Girnar Hill. To reach the summit there are 2000 steps. On the top there is a temple called Amba Matar where newlyweds worship, hoping that by so doing they will have a happy and fruitful

48 Girnar Hill, Junagadh

marriage. Fifty-four kilometres (34 miles) away, and a day's excursion, is the Gir Forest, home of the Asian lion, though there are now less than 200 there. Touring around is done by jeep.

Porbander
The birthplace of Mahatma Gandhi and an attractive summer resort by the Arabian Sea, the main industry here is fishing. One would need to be over in West Saurashtra to make a visit here worthwhile.

Rajkot
On a direct air route from Bombay, Rajkot is the most centrally situated town in Saurashtra. It is easily accessible by rail or by road but the air connection has obvious advantages. It is a picturesque city blending the old and the new. There are two beautiful lakes and a park and one of the best public schools in India. Nearby is Wankaner Palace where, with the permission of His Highness, one can stay as a paying guest and enjoy swimming in the pool and living in style.

Dwarka
Again over in the far west, but important because of its place in Hinduism, Dwarka is among the seven most holy places of pilgrimage for the Hindus, being associated with Lord Krishna, hero of the Mahabharata.

Palitana
Noted for its holy hill called Shatrunjaya, meaning 'place of victory'. From the top of Palitana there is a 2 km (1 mile) walk to the start of the ascent which climbs 600 m (1968 ft) to the hill top. Over a period of 900 years, 863 temples have been built here. The sight is staggering and awesome and the views over land and seas from the top are marvellous. Almost all the temples are Jain and, as the hill top is dedicated exclusively to the gods, when dusk falls even the priests depart. Tours can be arranged from nearby Bhavnagar or from Ahmedabad.

Kutch
This westernmost part of Gujarat is almost completely covered with water during the monsoon season, eventually giving way to marsh and salt flats as the waters recede. During the hot season this area turns into a vast expanse of dry mud. When flooded by both sea water and river water, the Kutch becomes a breeding place for flamingos and pelicans. The major town of Kutch is Bhuj, an old walled city that, until recently, closed its gates to travellers at 8.30 each evening. One can get to this strange and remote area by air either from Bombay or Rajkot, and one can travel there by rail and road.

Chorwad
A holiday complex that has recently been up-dated by the Gujarat

49 The abode of the Jain Gods at Palitana, Gujarat

Tourist authorities, Chorwad is situated on the south coast of the State. There are holiday cottages and bungalows, a swimming pool and facilities such as reading rooms and the inevitable video-movie shows.

Chorwad's principal feature is the palace, once the summer residence of the Nawabs of Junagad. The palace is an imposing building of turreted towers and deep porches concealing elegant rooms fitted out as they were left, in cubic thirties style with aggressive fireplaces, high doors and paned windows.

Indian Airlines runs a daily service from Bombay to Keshod, 38 km (24 miles) from Chorwad, making this resort an attractive weekend away for those with the time.

Chorwad is also a convenient place from which to visit the Gir Forest, Somnath and Diu.

Maharastra

Maharastra was once a part of a much greater region called Bombay Province but, because of the social and linguistic differences between the Gujaratis and the Marathas, this large area, of which Bombay was the capital, was split, thus creating the States of Gujarat and Maharastra.

Along with linguistic differences there was also the feeling amongst the Marathas that they did not get the work opportunities in Bombay that the Gujaratis enjoyed. The problem was really more involved, both socially and politically, but, for the purposes of this brief introduction, suffice it to record that the separation of Bombay Province was effected in May 1960, with Bombay becoming the capital of Maharastra, and Ahmedabad (later succeeded by the new city called Gandhinagar) becoming the capital of Gujarat.

Bombay

Once a struggling fishing village called Mumbai, Bombay has grown to become one of the world's greatest sea ports. It is the financial centre of India and an important industrial area, yet in spite of its heavy load of both people and business it manages to retain its attractiveness. It is a cosmopolitan city with a character of its own and no other place in India is in any way like it. Over-population brings with it the eternal problems of over-crowding and dirty streets but these conditions can be seen in other countries and, bearing in mind Bombay's problems, the city copes incredibly well.

In 1534 the Sultan of Gujarat ceded Mumbai to the Portuguese and in 1661 the King of Portugal gave the territory to Britain as a part of the dowry of Catherine of Braganza on the occasion of her marriage to Charles II. In 1665 the British took over all that part of the coast that was composed of islands. This stretched from Colaba in the south to Mahim in the north, including Mumbai, and in 1668 the British Government leased all seven islands to the East India Company for the trifling sum of £10 per year, to be paid in gold.

Perhaps the most important thing to happen to Bombay in those early years was the arrival of the Parsee community, which settled there in 1670. With their fine minds for business and language the community soon grew and became successfully established alongside the British. The two cultures were similar and to this day the Parsees have a strong attachment to the British and Britain.

Bombay has, though, a little of everyone from everywhere and all communities contribute to making it the colourful city that it is. There is the beautiful harbour studded with hilly islands, palm-fringed and accessible by boat – Elephanta Island being the most noted. There are also such features as the 'Queen's Necklace', a wide semi-circular carriageway curving from Nariman Point round to the Hanging Gardens of Malabar Hill which, at night, glitters like a rope of diamonds.

The Gateway of India, set beside the Taj Mahal Hotel and built to

50 Skyscraper Bombay showing the circular State Government building
beyond which are the dome and tower of the Taj Mahal Hotel

commemorate the visit to India of King George V and Queen Mary in
1911, saw its last official British occasion when, amidst pomp, splendour
and tears, Lord Mountbatten sailed away from India from the Gateway
after he had signed the Declaration of Independence; a token sailing
really, as his boat circled the bay and landed elsewhere so that he could
take a car out to the airport and fly back to England!

The fort area is the main commercial part of Bombay and around there
will be found the travel and shipping agents and all the banks. Along the
rocky ridges that make up the lower slopes of Malabar Hill live the well-
to-do residents, once in graceful houses; but this area is gradually being
developed so that it increasingly bristles with high-rise flat blocks. On the
top of Malabar Hill the Parsees built their Towers of Silence where their
dead are lain to be consumed by vultures. This is not a tourist spot and
great care is taken not to invade the privacy of the place. For the really
curious there is a model of the towers in the Prince of Wales Museum, but
imagination should be enough to explain their working.

Among thousands of interesting artefacts, the Prince of Wales Museum
has one of the finest collections of Moghul miniature paintings of which
one can buy very good reproductions. Nearby one can visit the Jehangir
Art Gallery and view the ever-changing exhibitions of painting and
sculpture. There is a good aquarium along Marine Drive and, for those
interested, a fine race-course.

For those interested in shopping for food, Crawford Market will provide all the spices imaginable plus a thousand other items. A porter will carry around all you buy, a service for which you will be thankful in the humid heat and for which you will gratefully tip the odd rupee before sinking into a taxi. The porter is useful in another way as he will know just where everything can be bought – silk scarves, cotton by the length, carved sandalwood etc.

The nearest beach for any reasonable swimming is at Juhu, about a half an hour by train from Bombay. Here are all the facilities offered by expensive hotels, plus the freedom to roam along the dun-coloured sands and watch as boys bury themselves alive in the sand, breathing through a straw, or the incredible-to-a-Westerner sight of Indian ladies bathing with all their clothes on!

Visit the Krishnagiri Upavan National Park, with the Kanheri Caves and the lakes from where Bombay gets most of its water. There is a huge open-air cinema before the entrance to the park. The names of the lakes are Powari, Vihar and Tulsi. The Kanheri Caves number 109 so one must be a dedicated visitor to make the visit worthwhile.

The tourist bus makes two excursions daily round Bombay and is an excellent way of seeing as much as possible in a short time; the Tourist Bureau near Church Gate Station has good maps and guide books of the city and surrounding areas.

Lonavala

Nearly 100 km (62 miles) south-east of Bombay, Lonavala lies up in the Western Ghats. It is a famous camping place and has bungalows and lakes and many walks. It is ideal for picnics in the hot weather and is a convenient stop-over en route for Poona (or, as it is now signposted and renamed, Pune, pronounced Poonay). There are the pre-Christian caves of Karle and Bhaje near Lonavala, but time there would be better spent in walking. Go midweek, if possible, because at the weekends the place is crowded with Bombay-ites escaping the heat.

Poona

The 'Deccan Queen' train takes about three hours from Bombay to reach Poona. The journey is 192 km (119 miles) and can also be made by air-conditioned bus or by sharing a taxi. The town lies 564 m (1850 ft) above sea level and has an all the year round bracing climate. Bracing, in the Indian context, means that there is a wind; that the wind may be hot and searing still entitles it to be thought of as bracing, for any movement of air in the hot weather is refreshing! There are many schools at Poona and a barracks. There are palaces and parks and one of the best race-courses in India. See the Raja Kelkar Museum, the Shanwarwada Palace, the Empress Gardens with fine tropical trees, and the Bundh Gardens on the banks of the river. The Aga Khan's palace is now a memorial to Mahatma Gandhi's wife, Kasturba.

Mahabaleshwar

Mahabaleshwar, at 1371 m (4500 ft) above sea level, is onwards from Poona. It is the highest hill station of the Western Ghats; founded in 1828, it was formerly the summer seat of the Bombay Government.

There are long walks through enchanting woods and glades and from many viewpoints spectacular views can be seen. The Panchgana Temple is said to contain the 'five streams', one of which is believed to be the source of the Krishna River; and there is a fort to explore. Some 20 km (12 miles) away is Panchgani, a minor hill station now noted for its private schools, one of which particularizes in the teaching of Arab sons from the Gulf regions. Modern development is spoiling much of this area.

Aurangabad

Aurangabad is an hour's flight from Bombay and is the most convenient point for visiting both the famous Ajanta Caves and the temples of Ellora. Apart from the mausoleum of the Rabia-ud-Durani, the wife of the Emperor Aurangzeb, there is little to see at Aurangabad. The justification for going is to see Ellora and Ajanta.

Ellora and Ajanta

The monuments of Ellora are of Buddhist, Hindu and Jain origin. Excavated in the scarp of a large rocky plateau, they are remarkable examples of stone carving. The most incredible is the rock-cut temple of Kailasa which is hewn out of one solid rock. Its massive pillars and colonnades, finely carved galleries and painted ceilings make it one of the wonders of the world. It is estimated that the task of quarrying the 85,000 cu. m (3 million cu. ft) of rock that were cut away must have taken no less than 100 years.

The Ajanta Caves are different altogether. They are set in a graceful curve on a hillside at the bottom of which runs a rushing river. The caves of Ajanta pre-date those of Ellora and are excavated in a wall of nearly perpendicular rock. Cut into the rock face are 29 caves of differing dimensions and interest. They date from around 200 BC to AD 650. Small guide books are available there, and small guides, little boys, will take the traveller around; strong legs are certainly needed. For those who wish there are 'dolly' chairs, like palaquins, in which one can be carried along by two or four strong sure-footed men.

Matheran

This is the nearest hill station to Bombay, 171 km (106 miles) from the city. The name means jungly wooded headland, which ideally describes the region with its undulating hills covered in trees. To get there you take the Bombay–Poona train and get off at Neral and then take the narrow gauge toy-train up the 21 km (13 miles) track to the top. The train winds and twists and people jump on and off, vendors sell drinks and sandwiches as the train is moving and the journey is great fun, taking about two hours to Matheran. With its lakes and waterfalls, Matheran is a convenient detour from Bombay – April, May and June being the best times to go.

Madhya Pradesh

The State of Madhya Pradesh came into being on the 1st of November 1956, nine years after Independence. In a comparatively short time, though, it has become a not unpowerful voice in Central Government in Delhi.

One large industry is Gwalior Suiting, material famous throughout India which can be seen advertised on hoardings and walls everywhere. The State produces coal, manganese-ore and copper, and a tobacco called *tendu patta* which yields the leaves from which a great proportion of the *bidis*, the small cheroot-type cigarette smoked ubiquitously over India, are made. Another unusual crop is sal seed, used as a cocoa-butter in producing chocolate.

Madhya Pradesh is the largest State in India, being nearly as large as France. It has a population of over 52 million. The scenery is very grand, full of gorges and forest and high areas such as the Vindhyas and the Satpuras, two mountainous regions amongst which rise the rivers Narmada and Tapti. This whole region forms the backdrop for the Jungle Book stories of Rudyard Kipling. In the forests live such tribals as the Gonds, the Bhils (migrants from Rajasthan) and the strange and docile Oraons and Korooks.

Soapstone, marble, quartz, sandstone, corundum . . . the list of minerals to be found in the State is long indeed, but perhaps the most romantic is diamonds. Though not found in large quantities, diamonds are dug for in the district of Panna. I am told, though, that the physical exercise of digging for them would benefit a prospector more than would the financial return from his harvest!

Due to the vastness of the State there are still places which are unknown to Indian travellers let alone to foreign visitors. Certainly the package tour operators seldom operate away from the more obvious places such as Khajuraho, with its erotic carvings, or Sanchi with its Buddhist associations; both have become major attractions. The State abounds, though, in off-beat places that are easily accessible if a little trouble is taken – places like Orchcha or Mandu or the Bagh Caves – and it is comparatively easy to plan such a tour providing arrangements are put in hand well in advance.

In the seventh century AD, central India formed a great part of the empire of the ruler Harsha, a warrior king who once conquered most of northern India. The period from AD 300 to the death of King Harsha in AD 647 is known as the 'Golden Age' of the Guptas.

Hiuen Tsang, a Chinese traveller and historian of those times wrote that 'the great warrior Harsha could put into the field ready for battle, 60,000 elephants and 100,000 cavalry'. It is incredible to think not only of the management of such a vast array but of the sheer space the assemblage would occupy. Hiuen Tsang relates another side to Harsha, that 'he used to distribute all the treasure accumulated by him (battle trophy) among the poor and he was once so impoverished that he had to ask his sister for a garment for his own use'. Whatever the truth, there is no doubt that Harsha was a great ruler. Where there is doubt is over the actual destinies of the central area of India from the death of Harsha to the coming of the Moghuls in the twelfth century.

For three centuries, until the Moghuls took the throne of Delhi, Hindu and Muslim rulers fought each other for supremacy.

During British times, central India comprised a large number of small (some very small) and large princely States together with British governed territory, until, after Independence, the Old Central Provinces became present-day Madhya Pradesh.

Bhopal

The capital of Madhya Pradesh, Bhopal's early history goes back to Raja Bhoj in the eleventh century AD. The foundations of the present city were not laid until the early part of the eighteenth century.

There are two picturesque lakes – the Great Lake, 15 sq. km (6 sq. miles) in area from which a bridge leads to the Lower Lake. The city is built around these lakes, alongside which a hill called Shimla rises 152 m (500 ft) and from the top of which there is a panoramic view of the city, especially at night when it is lit up. The bazaars here are some of the most fascinating in India.

Bhopal has more recently acquired an undesirable fame as the site of the Union Carbide plant gas leak in 1984 which killed and maimed thousands of people. The effects of this disaster will last for generations.

Gwalior

A principal sight in Madhya Pradesh is Gwalior. Only in recent years has it been considered by tour operators, yet it is easily accessible from either Delhi or Agra.

Gwalior Fort, set 91 m (300 ft) up on an extensive escarpment, dominates the city. Its honey-coloured sandstone, glowing in sunshine and glittering in the rains, still has remnants of the original inlaid tile-work of blue, green and yellow. Seen from below the elephant gateway and its six great dome-capped towers are an impressive sight.

The fort was started by a Rajput chieftain named Suraj Sen in gratitude to one Gwalipa, a hermit and ascetic who lived on top of the hill. The hermit cured Suraj Sen of leprosy by giving him a drink of water from a blessed tank, called today the Suraj Kund. The Tomar King, Man Singh (1486–1516), built the six-towered Man Singh Palace, considered to be the noblest specimen of Hindu domestic architecture extant in India. He also built the Gujari Mahal for his queen. This palace nestles at the foot of the hill directly below the Man Singh and is now a museum. In 1784

51 The Man Singh Palace, Gwalior – elephants ride to the main gate, *c.*1910

the Maratha King Madhu Rao Scindia took the fort and established his dynasty, during which the fort played a key role in the Mutiny of 1857.

Although the then Maharajah remained loyal to the British, his troops did not. The Gwalior contingent of nearly 18,000 men, commanded by one Tantia Tope, a brilliant Maratha General, and assisted by the legendary Rani Lakshmi Bai of Jhansi (India's Joan of Arc), led the fight against the British. The British had annexed the kingdom of Jhansi, some miles south of Gwalior after the Raja, Gangadhar Rao died (1853) without leaving a son. His widow, the Rani of Jhansi, swore undying vengeance against the British and assumed leadership of the freedom-fighters. On June 17th, 1858, she was slain leading her troops against a charge by the British cavalry. There is a splendid cenotaph to her memory about 2 km (1 mile) from Gwalior railway station.

The area up on the hill is 5 km (3 miles) long and 2 km (1 mile) wide in places, and you will need more than one day to do justice to all that there is to see. It is wise to arrange to spend a night in one or other of the good hotels in Gwalior – the Usha Kiran Palace, for instance.

Many of the bungalows and barracks seen all around the fort were built by the British, the main group now being used as one of the larger public schools in India, the Scindia School, founded in 1898.

Jhansi and Orchcha
Though actually in Uttar Pradesh by a hairsbreadth, it is better to mention Jhansi here in the context of Gwalior. It is 100 km (62 miles) south of Gwalior and, though there is little to see in Jhansi town, only

11 km (7 miles) away is the fortress palace of Orchcha, an easy ride by local rickshaw. The palace is beautifully situated on the banks of the Betwa River. The ceilings and walls of the Raja Mahal and the Laxmi Mandir show fine examples of Bundela paintings, some of which were destroyed by the cooking fires of the British troops. Part of the palace has been converted into a rest house and to stay overnight is a magical experience. Orchcha is medieval and is a quite different aspect of India accessible to all but the hasty traveller.

Sanchi

In 1818 a British officer rediscovered the Buddhist site of Sanchi. It was one of those accidental happenings like that which led to the discovery of Ajanta. Nothing was done to restore the site until 1881 when treasure-trove hunters were more to be seen than actual restorers. Eventually Sir John Marshal organized the repair of the structures to their present-day condition. It is interesting to reflect upon how much of the world has been restored, reclaimed, rebuilt and generally looked after by people foreign to the land.

At Sanchi one notices how clean everything is and how quiet the surrounding area. The Great Stupa, or memorial shrine, is situated on a hill. It was built by the Emperor Asoka in the third century BC, the original brick stupa now being enclosed in a stone one.

Khajuraho

The temples of Khajuraho were built between AD 950 and AD 1050 around the time of the Norman Conquest. The dynastic rulers were the Chandellas, who worshipped Lord Vishnu. Later rulers built temples to Shiva and there is evidence of the existence of Jain temples. The museum here houses a colossal statue of Buddha, which was found outside the Ghantai temple.

Each temple stands on a high base of solid masonry with a terrace around. Tall and spire-like, the temples lead from outer porticos to inner sanctums, where the idols are housed. The temples are famous for their beauty of outline and the complexity of the surface decoration. They are covered with a galaxy of gods and goddesses, serpents and hand-maidens, heavenly beauties, foliage and trees, and erotic representation. To the ancient devout, sexuality was symbolic of man's union with the divine, with the life source; it was not thought of as stimulatory. Some believe that the sculptures were a test of the singlemindedness of the devout pilgrims who came to pray. Whatever the reason for their being there, they underline, by their proximity to, and involvement with, religious ceremony, that sex is a part of life to be enjoyed for the continuation of life and not, as some would have it, to be seen either as an uncontrolled pleasure or a necessary evil.

Khajuraho is in an odd position to have flourished for so long. There is a half-hearted lake relying on the monsoons to keep it filled, but the nearest river is far away and one wonders, unless the terrain was vastly different, how a work force of artisans assembled to build the temples was fed and watered. Yet there must have been enough water, for the Chandellas ruled for 500 years.

Ujjain

It is believed that it was at Ujjain that Lord Shiva, God of destruction, vanquished the demon Tripura. Ujjain therefore is a very holy place for the Hindus. As at Allahabad, every twelve years a Kumbh Mela is held when millions of the devout descend on the city to bathe in the river Sipra. If you are travelling in the area in 1992/3 then be prepared for the immense crowds, for it is then that the next Kumbh Mela will be.

Indore

Indore has a fascinating and beautiful attraction right in the centre. This is the Manch Mandir, a shrine to the sect of Jains called Digamber Jains. The walls, roof, floor and doorways of this shrine are covered with mother-of-pearl inlay, glass beads and mirror-work and realistic paintings illustrating the punishments suffered in the next world by those who sin in this world. It is fascinating because of the patience and diligence of the workers who built it, and beautiful as a result of years of care.

Other than this attraction, Indore has little to see. There is the rather dull Palace of the Holkars, the ruling family of Indore and some none too interesting bazaars.

Pachmari

At an altitude of 1100 m (3609 ft) Pachmari has a bracing climate all the year round. The hills encircle a plateau over which the action of the elements has carved fantastic shapes in the red sandstone of the area. There are groves of trees which seem always to be in bloom, and attractive walks and bridle paths. It is quite unlike any other hill station in India – softer and warmer and, if possible, quieter; it is famous for its delicious wild bee honey. The rains last from June to September and are the secret of the hundreds of waterfalls and rivulets that traverse the countryside. Dhupgarh is the finest peak from which to view the Bori Valley (1350 m [4428 ft]).

At Pachmari there are bathing pools, a golf course, tennis and badminton and, at the Pachmari Club, there is a good library. Tourists can enrol as temporary members.

Mandu

Mandu spreads over a plateau 609 m (2000 ft) high in the Vindhya Mountains, in central India. It is on the western edge of the State of Madhya Pradesh.

All around, the country is rugged jungle scarred with deep ravines which run for miles. They guide the monsoon waters towards the

Chambal or Narmada, two great rivers of central India.

In October and November, after the monsoons have ceased, everywhere is lush and green. There are acres of land available for grazing cattle and goats. Fields are hedged by flowering mallow, and mud banks form wallows for leathery buffaloes.

The Chambal rises nearby – a stream which fast becomes a force capable through time of gouging out a valley 152 m (500 ft) deep, where water gushes and falls through rock fissures. Everything seems larger than life. Trees have leaves like elephants' ears, forced by the shortness of the season to breathe fast and conserve resources for the coming drought. Most bear fruit quickly, which ripens and falls into the cracked mud below, where it awaits the next year's rains.

At this time, on the roads to Mandu, the labourer, the goatherd and the oxherd fatten with the season's plenty. All too soon these tough people will thin down, to an existence which will make them deny water to a thirsty traveller, so far do they have to fetch it for themselves.

Approaching the Vindhyas one sees the mass of flat-topped mountains upon which Mandu lies. The road winds through stone-walled hill farms and eventually around a series of hairpin bends leading to four gateways, the last of which, the Delhi Gate, is flanked by a broad elephant ascent – wide grass-covered stone steps rising to a high arched entrance.

The hilltop area is 21 sq. km (8 sq. miles) – a considerable patch of land, yet most of the corners have at one time been the site of buildings. Tombs and chattries and pavilions scatter the landscape, their time-blackened domes and pillars blending romantically with foliage and flower. Now crumbling, they once honoured the spirits of past warriors. Kings have more imposing tombs.

A great dome, seemingly supported by four surrounding smaller ones, covers the remains of Hoshang Shah (1405–1432). Black with age, the domes stand imposingly in the heart of the village of Mandu, inappropriately grand for their now humble surroundings. When new, glittering with tile work and precious stones, the sight of Hoshang Shah's tomb must have been impressive, for Shah Jehan sent architects to study its style before finally choosing the design for the Taj Mahal at Agra. Also nearby is the Jami Masjid, a mosque so large that it is difficult to imagine where the faithful came from to worship there. Of course there were pilgrims but it must have been inspired by a fervour that eventually outstripped its usefulness, except as an exaltation to Allah.

Most of the remaining buildings lie less than 1 km (½ mile) away and comprise a palace called the Jahaz Mahal – heart of the 'City of Joy', as Mandu was once known. This complex, together with all the buildings on the plateau, gives the impression of being built as much for defence as pleasure. You have to guard a reputation, especially one for harems, sport, decadence and joy. You also have to guard against envy. The Jahaz Mahal, with its pools of perfumed water, pierced marble work, sumptuous rooms, decorated architecture and, above all, the people who lived in privileged style there, was an obvious cause of envy, not least because of its setting between two lakes. Often referred to as the Ship Palace, it enjoys cool breezes from the waters for most of the year.

Muslim Mandu was pre-Moghul. It was founded as early as the eleventh century by the Parmar Kings, whose rule ended when the Khiljis of Delhi annexed Mandu in 1304. After 100 years Mandu declared itself independent of Delhi, defended itself and developed great architecture, the remains of which can now be seen. The Tower of Victory (fallen), the Hindola Mahal, the audience hall, the Jami Masjid and the Jahaz Mahal were all built in 1401–1540. Mandu then fell to the Gujarat Muslims.

The last independent ruler of Mandu was Baz Bahadur. Baz fell in love with a girl called Rupmati, a singer from, it is said, the banks of the Narmada. Plucked from obscurity and treated as a queen, she has become a legend in Indian historical lore. Baz built a palace for himself by a lake called Reva Kund, and nearby, on the crest of a hill, erected a huge pavilion, with shaded lower walks and two large domed kiosks. This pavilion overlooks distant ravines and forest, from 300 m (985 ft), and is breathtakingly beautiful, especially at sunset. Rupmati sang her songs and was loved by Baz. The end of this affair was iconoclastic; it was the end of independent Mandu as well as the end of the love affair. Akbar the Great attacked Mandu, captured it – some say it was the legend of Rupmati that inspired his effort – and the Moghul reign commenced. Defeated, Baz fled, leaving Rupmati to her fate – the arms of Akbar. She thwarted him by taking a lethal dose of poison.

Some of the buildings were destroyed by Akbar after taking possession, but Jehangir, who inherited Akbar's empire, repaired much of the damaged stone work and made beautiful additions to the Jahaz Mahal, including pierced screens and watery gazebos.

This was the last glorious period of Mandu. After the fall of the Moghul Empire, regional government returned to Mandu by way of the prosperous city of Dhar, 39 km (24 miles) away. It was Dhar which had provided most of the labour force with which to build Mandu, during the preceding 600 years, and it is fascinating to contemplate the perils and setbacks involved in building this large complex of palaces and temples. India must have been much the same, climatically, as it is now. Monsoons would have prevailed; lashing water would have halted building and washed away mixed mortar and fresh workings. Road communications would have been impossible for a third of the year. The immense effort of labour would have had to 'follow the whip' of feudal lords, who paid either in grain or promise. The womenfolk would have worked as they still do – carrying stone and mortar on their heads. The landscape was chipped clean of boulder and hillock. Baked clay, carved into extravagant geometric patterns, glazed tiling and wheeled stone embellished the mammoth frameworks. The pre-Moghul arch is similar to the Gothic Perpendicular. This gives some of the ruins, especially those over water stretches, the appearance of Fountains Abbey or Rievaulx.

Successive rulers protected their paradise, but at a cost. 'City of Joy' is an ironic, romantic epithet. It is easy to forget the means to the end. The city ought to be a testament not only to the imagination of emperors but also to the human force which created it.

Mandu is slowly becoming a tourist attraction to visitors from countries other than India. The register of the travellers lodge shows that the number of foreigners who go there each year, though still small, is gradually increasing.

The Mandu Plateau is populated by hardworking farmers. Their bright green or red turbans are tied so as to flop around the head for shade, and the womenfolk dress in vivid reds and yellows, mostly a loose-fitting sari, and sometimes with pantaloons. There are bullocks, cows and buffaloes. Before the drought season, the green hills abound with life, including apple-green beetles, flying foxes, butterflies, dragonflies and pied kingfishers. White herons peck at lizards and snails and the man-size sarus crane sometimes lands and lords it over all. When night falls, tiger, panther and jackal roam, and grunts and cries echo around the still palaces and temples as fireflies flit around the tombs.

Getting to Mandu is not easy for tourists bound by pre-arranged schedules. A day would not be sufficient unless the visitor were within easy reach of the site. Mandu is 97 km (60 miles) from Indore, which is 560 km (348 miles) north of Bombay and 800 km (497 miles) south of Delhi. Indore is connected to both cities by a good air service and by rail. Additionally, there are bus services from Indore. Beware of the country bus which visits surrounding villages, takes hours, and is crowded. The journey should take about two and a half hours, and the cost is minimal; alternatively, one can, of course, take a private taxi.

To be in too much of a rush would be to miss the essence of Mandu. At least one night should be spent there. Indian sunsets and sunrises are special everywhere, but at Mandu they are magical.

The name 'City of Joy' may not be exactly appropriate, in the historical sense, but for the visitor it is a fair representation of present-day Mandu.

Goa

There are still aspects of Goa which are unaffected by the mass of visitors, all of whom seem to congregate on two or three of the beaches.

Panaji, once called Panjim, is the capital and is a busy river inlet. It is here where the steamer arrives from Bombay, a novel way of reaching Goa. The sea journey attracts many of all nationalities and if you want peace and quiet to enjoy the Indian coast, then book first class.

Other than the sea route, the easiest way to get to Goa is by train from Bombay as you then arrive near the centre. If you go by air then the journey will be quicker, but both the airport at Bombay and the one at Goa are way out of the centre of things and much time and frustration can be experienced en route.

The Goanese beaches have become one of the world's focal points for the sun-seekers, much to the detriment of the once wild stretches of sea-swept dunes backed by palms. They have, alas, been built on and exploited until there is not much difference at some places between them and Marbella or Miami.

The surrounding ambience, though, cannot be destroyed. The Portuguese were a zealous and a jealous lot. They forbade the building of Hindu or Muslim shrines anywhere near the beaches of the coast, possibly to preserve fishing and trading rights, and consequently such centres of worship are to be found inland. This has been a blessing in disguise as they are now separate from the holiday hustle and bustle.

The interior in Goa is a paradise of emerald fields of rice surrounded by palms and mangoes. Settlements of white-painted houses nestle amongst

52 Township of Ponda, Goa, showing the quaint temple tower

the lush countryside, and townships like Ponda are engagingly attractive.

The most important Christian church is that called Bom Jesus, which houses the tomb of St Francis Xavier. Nearby is the Palace of the Inquisition, benign now under the Goan sun but once the scene of cruel imprisonment and torture – in the name of God.

Goan food has, over the years, developed into something which is unique, a mixture of East and West. Sea food is a staple diet and shrimps, crabs and lobsters are available throughout the year. There are oysters and mussels, when in season. Goan sausage, called *chourisso*, is delicious and good for taking on a picnic; *spartel*, made from the liver of the pig and cooked in spices is a delicacy. There is *sanna*, small steamed rice cakes fermented in *toddy*, and *bebinca*, a rich coconut pudding.

The Goans distil liquor from coconuts and the fruit of the cashew. Feni is the most popular of these. As with vodka, it too has no colour but it packs a powerful kick and seems to contribute to the good-hearted bibulous boisterousness of the locals.

Karnataka

Southern India is a very different place from the rest of the sub-continent.

53 The Vidhana Souda, Karnataka State's Government headquarters, an imposing example of architecture incorporating styles of the past, completed in the 1960s

When one gets south of Poona one can sense a difference – the crops change from the predominantly wheat-growing north to the rice of the south and the people are darker skinned with different features. They are of the original Indians, called Dravidians, once ousted from the north by the Aryans.

Relatively unaffected by the invasions and wars that shaped northern India, the south remains still (and nowhere more so than in the villages) India as it must have appeared to the early missionaries.

It is a fascinating region where ancient India can be seen as it was left by the kings of the south, the Pallavas, the Cholas and the Hoysalas.

Bangalore

In AD 1537 a ruler called Kempe Gowda cut a way through what was the jungle and found a stretch of country climatically near perfect, dotted by small lakes. It is said that he ordered four bullock carts to plough their way, with ploughshares, in four directions, and when they stopped out of exhaustion, Gowda had four conical towers constructed; they stand today as a historical reminder of the extent to which he expected his township to grow. Inside his fortifications various localities were separated into *pets*, or communal areas, each dealing in a different trade. Today one can wander through such districts as Chickpet, Balepet and Nagarpet – bazaars selling everything one can think of.

The salubrious climate of Bangalore has contributed greatly to its popularity. Situated at a height of 914 m (3000 ft) it has moderate temperatures conducive to green growth and lush parks – Cubbon Park and the Botanical Gardens being prime examples – to say nothing of tree-lined streets.

Once known as 'the pensioner's paradise', Bangalore has burgeoned into a city of 3 million, taking the overflow from cities like Bombay, Delhi, Baroda and Calcutta. It was recently described as a 'cocktail of peoples'. Outside Bombay it is certainly the most cosmopolitan city in India.

The silks of this area are famous all over the world. Apart from those indigenous to Karnataka, such as Bangalore and Mysore silk, the emporiums and bazaars stock silk from all over India which one can buy by the metre or as saris – wild silk, tussore silk, the China silks and silk from Benares and Kancheepuram are part of the selection available.

There is a move afoot by the Karnataka Silk Industry to endeavour to popularize the silk-worm pupae as a high protein food. In China, apparently, the custom of eating the pupae is age-old. One wonders, though, at the eating sensitivity of the people, for apart from any natural revulsion, they are mostly vegetarian, while the silk-worm pupae would be considered non-vegetarian.

Bangalore is an excellent centre from which to tour Karnataka. Trains and buses speed one to Mysore (two hours) and tours will take in most places of interest. There are cinemas galore, fine shops and excellent coffee houses and, above all, plenty of good company.

54 The enormous Nandi (Bull) at Chaumundi Hill, Mysore

Mysore

City of palaces and gardens and old bazaars and the residence of the Maharajah of Mysore. After Independence, the Maharajah was made Governor of the State of Karnataka, a recognition of his and his predecessors' accomplishments in the way of modernizing the then Mysore State.

Mysore is especially popular around October/November time when the festival of Dussara and Diwali is held (see Festivals and Fairs). Many people crowd into the city during this time and accommodation is hard to come by. One should try and secure hotel rooms well in advance, and also a place on the 'stands' from which to watch the Dussara procession of elephants. Then the spathodia trees will be in bloom, their large panicles of red flowers radiant against the sky; flowers will be everywhere and the city really looking its best.

At any other time Mysore is a quiet university city. There is a daily coach tour arranged by the local tourist bureau. It is fashionable to stay at the Krishnasagar Hotel at the Brindavan Gardens – beautiful, too, but these gardens are 19 km (11 miles) out of Mysore, and so not very convenient for seeing the city. The Wren-esque Lalita Mahal, once a palace and now a five-star hotel, is quite near the centre and is an unusually un-Indian sight in Mysore.

55 The impressive tomb of Mohammed Adil Shah, the Gol Gumbaz at Bijapur

Bijapur

This city is in northern Karnataka and accessible from Poona or from Sholapur. City of domes and minarets, Bijapur is a medieval walled city, almost wholly Muslim, whose main sight is the Gol Gumbaz, the enormous tomb of Mohammed Adil Shah, who ruled Bijapur in the seventeenth century AD. The dome of the tomb is 38 m (124 ft) in diameter, second only in size to the dome of St Peter's at Rome. Like all domes it is noted for its whispering gallery.

Bijapur is a garden township, pleasant and very Muslim. There is a feeling here of being in a different age, but alas there are few facilities. There is, though, a travellers' lodge and a KSTDC tourist home where all but the most fastidious would be comfortable.

From Bijapur one can visit the Hindu temples of Aihole and Badami, deep-set in a gorge, and one can go to Pattadakal and see the Chalukyan caves and temples. The conditions can be fairly primitive in this area. Few travellers come this way and local buses can be a problem, being always jam-packed with both people and animals!

Seringapatnam

This historic place lies on a small island in the River Cauvery. It was once the fortress of Tipu Sultan and, though little remains of the fort, the setting is beautiful. It is a popular place for Indians to go for picnics and to pray at the Ranganathaswamy Temple. Nearby, and probably the most important sight, is the Daulat Bagh Palace and the Gumbaz, Tipu Sultan's summer palace and mausoleum respectively. Almost the whole of

56 Tomb of Tipu Sultan
at Seringapatnam,
Mysore

the palace walls are covered in fine paintings depicting life at the palace
and in the battlefield, some of them surprisingly frank, resembling giant
Moghul miniatures.

Sravanabelgola, Belur and Halebid

At Sravanabelgola there is a monolithic statue of Lord Gomteswara, the
Jain saint. The naked giant stands 17 m (over 50 ft) tall and has been
there for a thousand years. Five hundred steps lead up to the top of the
hill on which stands the huge statue. Every twelve years thousands of Jain
pilgrims congregate here for the colourful festival called Mahamastakab-
hishekha, when the statue is anointed with milk and honey, vermilion
kumkum water, silver coins and curd.

From Sravanabelgola, Halebid and Belur are no more than an hour's
drive. Here are Hoysala temples in a sylvan setting with a profusion of
carving that is literally breathtaking. Using a form of soap-stone, the
designers carved every form of intricate pattern. The softness of the stone
gradually hardened with time, a testimony to their skill and to the 80
years of labour (eleventh- to twelfth-century AD).

57 Interior of Tipu Sultan's tomb, Seringapatnam, Mysore

58 The monolithic statue of Lord Gomteswara at Sravanabelgola – over 15 m (50 ft) tall

Vijayanagar

Vijayanagar is so incredible, so different an experience in India and so rewarding that it deserves a more detailed description. It is visited by comparatively few tourists, is unknown to many people, and yet is quite easy of access from either Bangalore (6 hours by car) or Bijapur (four hours by car).

The bus from Hospet, in the south Indian State of Karnataka, takes about 20 minutes to reach Hampi, travelling at first over a plain of cultivated fields with hills in the distance. After an abrupt turn the road becomes rocky and hedged in by boulders. This is the beginning of the ancient Tungabhadra river course where erosion has bared the earth of any growth other than grasses. The tin lizzie bus lurches towards a one in four decline with an 'S' bend in the middle, where enormous nut brown rocks tower overhead. In a crazy hit and miss way the bus manages to run the course and grind to a halt in the main and only street of Hampi and it is from here, an unprepossessing one-horse shack street of cafes and pen shops and trumpery vendors, that one commences exploring the great Vijayanagar capital.

At one end of the street a huge carved gopuram (gateway) leads into the Pampapati temple complex and, at the other end, beyond the bus-stop, ghost-ways run up into the nearby hills and to the remains of the inner fortified walls. Below the south side of the main street the Tungabhadra river has carved a deep ravine and water cascades over boulders and rocks. People wash and swim and pray there and, on the far side, green plantations, a guest house and farms lead the eye through ruins to hazy hills. All around are ruined buildings, their roofs missing and grass growing from their structure. Roadways lead nowhere and are littered with fallen pillars and half buried figures. Tracks are covered with scrub which disguises the order they once gave to the houses of tradesmen and also to temples, palaces and gardens. Throughout the 155 sq. km (60 sq. miles) the feeling is Pompeian but with a difference, as the visible destruction was made by man not by nature.

The affairs of north India in the fourteenth century were turbulent indeed, and in 1398 Tamberlain the Great sacked Delhi. Peninsular India south of Bombay was a boiling pot of Muslim machinations against Hindu rule. All coastal regions were open to trade with foreign entrepreneurs eager for spices and staple products such as rice and cotton, and local potentates were not slow to expand their fortune by a process of export and import.

Elsewhere in the world in 1327 the Aztecs were building Tenochtitlan, now Mexico City, and in 1368 the Ming dynasty was founded.

Around 1336 the rule of the Sultanate of Delhi stretched southwards over the Deccan to beyond what is now Maharashtra, and aimed at dominance of the south. Some nobles overlording tracts of country in the south became jealous of Delhi's appointment of 'Amirs', personal representatives, and in areas such as Malwar and Gujarat and the Deccan

59 View over Vijayanagar and valley, carved out by the Tungabhadra River; the Pampapati Temple is in the foreground

this jealousy led to a cohesion of diverse interests, actively against the Sultan of Delhi. They formed what were known as 'centurions' to guard local interests, adding to the difficulties of political rule of the Deccan and south, a huge region in central and southern India.

In spite of this the Sultan managed to maintain some stability and there was no open defiance of Delhi's rule. Then one Ashan Shah, inspiring a new confidence, organized a successful revolt and ignited the smouldering embers of disaffection. Eventually there was a flare-up and insurrection which resulted in the Deccan empire of the Sultan being reduced to a shambles. Gujarat, Malwar and Sindh followed suit and, in an attempt to restore order, the Sultan, Mohammed I, lost his life.

About this time, two of five sons of a local Hindu potentate were captured and taken to Delhi where they were forcibly converted to Islam, which included circumcision. They were seen as suitable pawns to utilize in suppressing further risings in the south. One was Harihar, who was sent as an executive, directly responsible to Delhi, and the other, his brother Bukka, became a minister and later army commander.

When the news of their appointment reached the south the local insurgents were filled with joy as they regarded the two men as political victors over the foreigners (Muslims) who were keeping them under rule.

Harihar had promised the Sultan that he would only exercise power as his vassal and he proceeded to act with prudence and wisdom, preserving his original Hindu identity and yet satisfying the Delhi Muslims by sending gifts to the Sultan. In this way he had little trouble with his territory and enjoyed comparative peace.

Then he came under the spell of a local Saint called Madhava Vidyaranga and it was he who organized Harihar's reacceptance amongst the Hindus – a difficult task, as, having been forced to become a Muslim, he had to regain caste within Hinduism. Vidyaranga was the only man who had the power to make this possible and acceptable to the people. Harihar appointed the Saint his Chief Minister (politics being then very much what they are today!) and, as minister, Vidyaranga advised the founding of a township to enshrine Hinduism. This was eventually called Vijayanagar and Harihar became King of Hastinavati, now called Hampi.

With his new duality, Harihar organized his military forces on an efficient and equable Muslim–Hindu basis and within five years (1341) had established his authority over the Konkan and Malabar area, with their ports, and also over the Tungabhadra river basin, which gave him fantastic water supplies for irrigation purposes. He is regarded as the first ruler of the Vijayanagar empire, with its great city at Hampi.

There were two principal kingdoms in south India at that time. One was Vijayanagar and the other was the kingdom of Bahmani, the latter being north of the River Krishna. The two kingdoms were permanent enemies, Vijayanagar being predominantly Hindu and Bahmani Muslim. Throughout the next 150 years the Bahmani rulers constantly attacked Vijayanagar but were never powerful enough to gain supremacy and occupy the territories south of the Krishna. More often than not these border wars resulted in an expansion of the Vijayanagar empire.

Harihar died in 1406 and his brother Bukka in 1408. Bukka had meanwhile organized Vijayanagar's defences, destroyed the neighbouring kingdom of Madura, and only after losing 400,000 men did he capitulate and honour a peace treaty with the Muslims. The two brothers had inherited the traditions of the old Hoysala dynasty, those of hostility to Islam and the glorification of Hinduism and they left this antagonism as their legacy.

Between 1346 and 1505 Vijayanagar, though constantly fighting Islam, consolidated its gains, developed its power and added to its immense wealth. In 1505 Krishna Deva Ray rose to power and, because of his personal strength and diplomacy, became the greatest of the rulers of Vijayanagar; indeed Babar referred to his 'giant powers' and praised his rule. Great men sometimes become conceited, and Krishna Deva Ray was no exception. His confidence in his power caused him to be politically careless, reversing, as he did, earlier benefits won from the Muslims for the Hindus. After his death he was succeeded by Rama Raja, a minister from a district called Sadashwa. Rama Raja was obstructive and destructive to neighbouring Muslim States and made enemies easily.

The city by then had seven fortified walls, one within the other, and beyond the outer wall was an esplanade 46 m (150 ft) deep into which stones had been fixed near to one another, the height of a man, so that neither foot nor horse could advance near the outer wall.

Domingo Paes visited Vijayanagar in 1502 at the height of its glory and described it as being as large as Rome, containing more than 100,000 houses. There were lakes and water courses and orchards. He found 34 shops in one corner of the palace enclave devoted to jewellery making and saw one room built entirely of ivory: 'all of ivory, the pillars and cross timbers all of ivory, carved with roses and lotus and other flowers'. All the utensils of the palace were of gold and silver, some gold vessels being of immense size.

The Raja family were great scholars who patronized Sanskrit and Telegu literature and encouraged poets and singers and painters. Rama Raja, over-confident because of success, went into battle, the great battle of Talikota (1565), but was unprepared for, and unable to quell, the united forces of Bidir, Ahmadnagar, Bijapur and Golkonda. He was defeated and killed and his severed head was raised on a spear for all the Hindus to see.

The victorious Muslims marched upon Vijayanagar and remained in possession of the once thought impregnable city, and they looted and devastated everything in sight. Vijayanagar, that was once so magnificent, with its huge temples, exquisite palaces and artisans of every sort, armouries, stables and vast piazzas for public worship was reduced to a shambles. Where once there were as many as 600,000 soldiers, where 24,000 horses were maintained at any one time and where stables were provided for 5000 elephants, little or nothing was left intact.

Bad news travelled fast and Rama Raja's brother, Tirumalia, escaped with much treasure loaded 'on 1550 elephants'. As the victorious army

60 The remains of the elephant stables at Vijayanagar

marched into the city, panic spread. Retreat was impossible, as was flight. Besides the army there came into the city tribal people, long separated from city life and having jealousies of their own; they too robbed and looted. Day after day they and the invaders continued their work of destruction and wrought havoc on the splendid city. Wealthy, industrious and prosperous one day, the next 'it was pillaged and reduced to ruins amid scenes of savage massacre and horrors beggaring description' (Sewell).

The main source of revenue for the Vijayanagar empire was a land tax. After this came tax on professions and on industry such as wheelwrights, potters and armourers. Marriage was also taxed, as were temple revenues. Vijayanagar was a shrine to Hinduism as opposed to Islam, and religious revenues must have been great indeed when one sees the profusion of shrines and temples.

Some of the goods traded in, as recorded, are: gold, silver, elephants from Ceylon, horses, velvet and satins from China and damask from Aden. Exports included rice, sugar, henna dye and indigo, sandalwood, pepper, cloves, cinnamon and cotton. As well as trading with the West, by 1565 trade with China was also flourishing. The Ming dynasty, founded in 1368, about the same time that Harihar had set Vijayanagar on the map of south India, was by 1570 nearing its last glories, and Chinese blue and white porcelain, jade ware, and ivory were traded throughout the Asian seas. As recently as April, 1980, broken pieces of China ware were unearthed at the ruins at Hampi and this find provided the first archaeological evidence of the ancient trade links between China and Vijayanagar.

Archaeologists stumbled upon potsherds of China ware which bore Chinese characters and miniature figures of men dressed in contemporary fashion. Other finds during this dig were of ivory finials and lead vessels. These excavations, which are a continuing process, will eventually reveal more evidence of trading connections with China; it is known that China, at this time, had large and powerful ships. So, of course, did Spain and the Dutch and British, all of whom had trading ports around the Indian coast by the middle of the sixteenth century.

To relate with other world events this great civilization, with its own painting, much of which can be seen *in situ*, on existing roofs and walls today, with its sculpture and architecture, politics and economic order, one might go back to the Aztec civilization which was eventually conquered and sacked by Cortes in 1521. Europe had witnessed the burning of Joan of Arc, Chaucer had written *The Canterbury Tales*, Caxton had invented his printing machine, and Botticelli, Raphael, Leonardo and Michelangelo had expended their genius. Shakespeare was born and Elizabeth I was on the English throne, and in India the great Akbar ruled supreme throughout the north.

What does one see today? A very great deal and all of it easily understandable as a great city with its culture, business and spiritual life.

The Hindus built well and on a gigantic scale. Religious fervour was their spur and not even the Muslim fanatiscism destroyed the greatest of temple and domestic architecture.

There is the setting, too, on the south, or right, bank of the Tungabhadra river: the waters run around rocks that rear out of the river-bed like giant elephants, many of which have temples built upon them. The surrounding hills are covered by green sandalwood and ber trees and by mangoes and neem trees and flame of the forest. Cheetah and panther stalk the hills and, within the memory of the villagers, wild horses roamed the hills. The valleys grow rice and sugar, wheat and spices, as in the olden days, and the fields are irrigated by the Tungabhadra and its mighty modern dam. Wild scented grass grows over the hills and is harvested by the Lambanis, the tribal people who have settled in the area. This grass is processed by distillation, whereby rose-scented oil is obtained which is highly prized by the soap and perfume industry.

All around the views are magnificent, either of the Karnataka country or of Vijayanagar. Time is needed to do justice to this ancient city spread over 23 sq. km (9 sq. miles). One can spend a couple of nights in one of the hotels (very humble) that are situated in the tatty high street of Hampi. Here one can eat a variety of foods, the best being any that is vegetarian, and the cost is minimal. Also there is a government tourist bungalow.

Andhra Pradesh

Linguistically created out of the old Hyderabad State together with the Telegu speaking part of the old Madras Presidency, Andhra Pradesh stretches from the Deccan plateau down to the Coromandel coast on the Bay of Bengal.

One of the anomalies of modern times is that this area, whilst being one of the poorest in India, was nevertheless the seat of the man reputed to be the richest man in the world – the Nizam of Hyderabad. With present-day development programmes being successfully carried out, the State is gradually becoming more prosperous. It is an interesting State around which to travel, very beautiful, sometimes stark, with a long coastline that is quite without exploitation.

Hyderabad

Like Bijapur, Ahmedabad and Allahabad, Hyderabad is largely Muslim. Its vast spread contains the twin cities of Secunderabad and Hyderabad. It is an important Islamic cultural centre as well as being one of the few places in south India where Western culture such as plays, music and dance can be enjoyed.

A famous landmark in the old quarter is the Char Minar, a great triumphal arch having four towers – the Char Minar or minarets – up which one can climb to obtain fine views over the city and old bazaars.

61 The Char Minar, Hyderabad, thought to have been erected to
commemorate relief from a plague

Nearby is the principal mosque, the Mecca Masjid, said to hold 10,000
worshippers. It is built of stone which is richly decorated with plaster-
work.

One of the prides of Hyderabad is the Salar Jung Museum. This huge
building, erected by a Prime Minister of the Nizam, has a rather
unattractive exterior of pre-stressed concrete painted pink. Inside are
some 35,000 exhibits of porcelain, pottery, painting, jewellery, manuscripts and armoury, the like of which cannot be seen anywhere else in
India.

Near Hyderabad is Golconda, an attractive, haunting ruined city
constantly being threatened by industrial development. A visit to Hyderabad should include some time spent at Golconda, for it is unique. It was
sacked by Aurangzeb in 1687, the defeated Kutb Shahi, King of
Golconda, retreating to Bhagnagar, later to be renamed Hyderabad,
originally founded in 1589, by Muhammed Kuli.

A guide book is available at the entrance to the Fort of Golcondo which
will be a useful companion when wandering around. If you are lucky
there might be a performance of song or dance at night there, lit by
torches, and the moon. Tourist buses run out daily, about a half an hour's
journey, but one needs to be there at dawn or soon after to experience
Golconda's magic. Nearby, a walk away, are the Qutab Shahi tombs set
in beautiful gardens. These royal tombs are most photogenic.

Tirupathi
This is one of the richest temple complexes in India. For most south

62 Inside the Salar Jung Museum, Hyderabad

63 Royal tomb at Golconda, Hyderabad

Indians it is an essential pilgrimage place. The temple is 762 m (2500 ft) up among a range of tree-clad hills where mangoes and sandalwood and mahogany trees grow. The place abounds with souvenir shops and eating places. Foreign visitors are welcome to see the temple providing they go barefoot and do not smoke; but they cannot witness Hindu worship.

Tiruttani
South of Tirupathi, this is another hill shrine. Here there are 365 steps leading to the entrance and there is a constant stream of pilgrims.

Kalahasti
This temple stands on the banks of a small river beneath the Eastern hills and is full of holy men and sages performing yoga, seemingly unaware that there is another world.

Mangalagiri
This is in the Guntur district of Andhra Pradesh, and the home of the temple of Lakshminarasinah Swami which has the highest gopuram in the State, a truly impressive sight seldom seen by visitors.

Vizagapatnam
This is one of the major ports on the eastern coast of India and, once separate, but now almost a suburb of Vizagapatnam, is Waltair, a seaside holiday place, once called 'the Brighton of India'. Now, far from being a sleepy holiday township, Waltair is the home of the Andhra University, the coming of which increased the spreading of urban development. Away from these places the beaches are fine, sandy and quite unspoilt.

64 The gopuram of the temple of Lakshminarasinah Swami at Mangalagiri,
Andhra Pradesh

Kerala

Kerala is not quite as big as Switzerland in area. It runs down the western coast from Mangalore (in Karnataka) to the southern tip of India. Kerala is a strip of land never more than 160 km (100 miles) wide, yet it has one of the densest populations in India. The State was created in 1956 and was formerly known as Travancore. Little over a year after its independence, the State elected a communist government and, by so doing, made history by being the first place in the free world to accept communist control – a form of State government which has been in and out of power ever since.

Kerala is a highly literate State, probably because there has always been a preponderance of Western schools run by various churches in the State. This literacy has had a two-edged effect. It has created a literate and highly educated community which cannot find enough work to absorb its talent. One of the results of this, especially over the last ten years, has been the outflow of educated Keralans to the Gulf States, resulting in a steady flow back to Kerala of money undreamed of a short time ago. The consequence of this has been an abundance of nouveaux riches.

The translation of Gulf money into rupee-power has given to many families a prosperity which has even altered the marriage prospects of many. Businesses, hotels, land exploitation and temple-wealth are areas which benefit from this 'new money'.

To the visitor, though, these things will not be apparent. The State of Kerala is welcoming, beautiful, humid, exotic and a paradise.

A quarter of its area is covered by forest, above which are the coffee and tea plantations, leading to the Cardamon Hills. Below, on the fertile plains which border the coast, grow marvellous peppercorns and spices such as ginger, cumin and, of course, coconuts.

Twenty-five per cent of the 25 million population are Christian; consequently, as you travel through the enchanting scenery of palms and rice fields and temples, there are many well-maintained churches, often painted in sparkling white as a protection against the heat.

Trivandrum

The university city of Trivandrum is the capital of the State of Kerala. It is a sleepy, dusty place spread out over seven hills. It is the seat of State government and a popular residential place. There are temples, music programmes and exhibitions of dance, and also the interesting museum, the Napier Museum, with its curious many-gabled roof and decorated walls. The city is near some marvellous beaches, many visited by the numerous bus tours that traverse the region.

Kovalum Beach

You get what you pay for all over the world and at Kovalum comfort is

65 The Napier Museum, Trivandrum

sharply divided between the pampering five-star facilities in marvellous hotels, and slumming it along the beaches in rooming hutments. Kovalum has been advertised as a paradise on earth and, to cater for the demand of so many for a visit to paradise, the Kerala State Tourist Department has not only converted a palace into a hotel but has built (almost disguised by clever planning) a beautiful, palatial complex into the rocks just by the sea. Recently, though, the building of a mosque – with Gulf money no doubt – is causing communal stirrings and, more important for the visitor, loudspeaker noise by proclaiming from the building the words of Allah – a harsh and unnecessary exultation, in paradise.

66 View over Kovalum Beach showing hotel complex blending into the rocky spur

Cochin

Important as a port and railway junction, these activities are never much in evidence and Cochin is a good centre from which to tour the rest of the State.

In Cochin all cultures and religions have met for hundreds of years. It is very much a water place, of islands and inlets and backwaters, of naval and commercial docks, and its waters are lively with all sorts of nautical life.

In an area called Mattancheri there is an interesting Jewish colony. Its synagogue has a floor made entirely of hand-painted blue and white Cantonese tiles, each one a different pattern. The synagogue was built in 1586 and must once have served a quite large Jewish community; this though has dwindled to only a few – referred to as the White Jews of Cochin. At Mattancheri too can be seen the 'Dutch' palace. It was built in the sixteenth century by the Portuguese 'as a gesture of good will', really meaning a price for safe trading. The murals are astonishing and are only equalled by those at the summer palace of Tipu Sultan, near Mysore.

An organized tour by launch will take one to Willingdon Island where the Malabar Hotel is set on the tip amidst lovely gardens but from where, each time you go out, you will be obliged to take a ferry. The tour will also go to the island of Gundu where there is a large *coir* factory producing,

67 Interior of the Jewish Synagogue at Mattancheri, Cochin: the floor is of blue and white Cantonese tiles, and each one is different

68 Coir mats, made from coconut fibre

among other things, door-mats. Coir is coconut fibre and, after being dyed, is woven into many-patterned mats.

Fort Cochin, as opposed to the mainland which is called Ernakulum, is reputed to be one of the oldest European settlements in India, with the landing of Alberquerque in 1503. He brought with him five monks who built the first Christian edifice there, later to be named the Church of St Francis. This was the burial place of Vasco de Gama, whose remains were later returned to Portugal.

If you wish for real escape then stay out in the middle of the waters of the harbour, on Bolgatty Island, at the State Tourist Bungalow. The building was built by the Dutch in 1744 as the Governor's Palace and continued as the British Residency until 1947. It has old timbered ceilings

69 Bolgatty Island: the State Tourist Bungalow, once the Governor's Palace

and polished floors and curving staircases; enormous rooms and baths; and the sitting-room has, around its walls, framed Daniels prints of scenes of India. There is also a spacious garden with a nine-hole golf course.

If time is available, then visit such places as Craganore, where the first Christians landed and where the earliest church in India, AD 400, is reputed to be. Visit Alwaye, from where one can roam the beautiful Munar District in the Kanan Devan Hills (1371 km [4500 ft]) and go round some of the tea plantations. Higher still is the Animudi Peak, 2719 m (8890 ft) high, with magnificent views. Spend a night at Allepy and then take the backwater boat trip on to Quillon – the living may be primitive but the scenery is unique. Save time too for a visit to the Periyar Wild Life Sanctuary, where, from the comfort of launches one can watch bison and elephants and – they say – tigers.

Tamil Nadu

Tamil Nadu could be called the heartland of Dravidian culture. Once a part of the huge Madras State, Tamil Nadu kept and preserved its customs and lifestyle. Never conquered, and little influenced by outside culture either military or artistic, this huge area (336,698 sq. km [130,000 sq. miles]), with a population of nearly 50 million, developed slowly but surely, all the time preserving its Hinduism and its language. Tamil is reputed to be the oldest language in the world still used by millions, both in India and outside India in places like Sri Lanka and Indonesia.

The interior rises from the coastal plains to the hills among which are situated the famous hill stations of the south: Ootacamund, Coonoor, Kotagiri, Kodaikanal, Yercaud, etc. It is up in these hills, near the border region with Kerala, that red bananas grow. These are delicious, tasting somewhere between a peach, passion fruit and banana.

Through the plains run the great temple towns of Tamil Nadu: Madurai, Trichy, Tanjore, down to the south and Rameswaran. Fireworks and matches are two lethal cottage industries which, because of accidents, claim many casualties each year.

Life in Tamil Nadu is leisurely and traditional either on its wide beaches or up in the hills. Its richly woven silks are famous throughout the world.

Madras

Madras is the fourth largest city in India. It was the earliest important British settlement and today is the capital of Tamil Nadu and has the principal harbourage of south-east India.

In Madras, distances from one place to another are always long. The two main streets, Mount Road and Poonamalle High Road look reasonably close on a street map, yet are 2 km (1 mile) apart at some places. It is more often necessary to take transport as the heat can be so fierce. The lesser tree-lined avenues connecting these two highways have graceful

70 Tea pickers on Rajamally Estate near Munnar in the Kanan Devan Hills, Kerala

Victorian-Moghul buildings set within verdant grounds. One such is the Connemara Library, another, Spencer's Departmental Store, where low buttresses lead to high pinnacles and gothic windows that conceal a multiplicity of goods for sale from garden furniture to grenadine flavouring.

On the coast is the church of St Mary, set inside the grounds of Fort St George. It is the oldest Anglican church east of Suez; it was consecrated in 1680. There is a memorial tablet here to the memory of Elihu Yale, born in Boston, USA, who became an English merchant and eventually Governor of Madras. The tablet commemorates the 250th anniversary of the naming after him of Yale University and was put there by classmates of Chester Bowles (Yale 1924), who was twice American Ambassador to India. Robert Clive was married in St Mary's.

St Thome Cathedral is an insipid building of uninspired buttresses supporting an uninspired spire. The cathedral commemorates St Thomas, doubting Thomas, who came as a missionary to India and was martyred on a small hill near where Madras airport is now. Beyond St Thome there is the temple called Kapaleshwara, dedicated to Shiva, around which are many interesting bazaars.

Further south is Adayar, the headquarters of the Theosophical Society, set in tranquil gardens by the sea. One is reminded of Madame Blavatsky, or Annie Besant, who died in 1933, and her protégé, J. Krishnamurthy who eventually disassociated himself with the Society and established his own Foundations in America, England, Switzerland and India.

71 Kapaleshwara Temple, Madras

Egmore Station is a graceful building in the Victorian-Moghul style. It has domed towers and russet coloured stucco work, plus a very grand entrance. It is from here that one sets off south, to places like Pondicherry.

Interesting excursions can easily be arranged from the centre of Madras to most of the surrounding places.

The tourist buses, or coaches (enquire about video films en route!) go to Mahabalipuram – the shore temples sometimes referred to as the Seven Pagodas. These monolithic rock-hewn temples have been greatly eroded through their exposed position on the shore, but they have withstood over a thousand years of storms. Near the temples is 'Arjuna's Penance', a colossal sculptural frieze, relief-carved on the face of a gigantic rock. It is the world's largest *bas-relief*. It tells the story of Mother Ganges, the great river which starts in the Himalayas and is the scene of so many mythological stories. There are animals and gods and flying creatures that, especially in the long shadowy light of early morning, seem to be actually moving.

Kancheepuram

In AD 640 the Chinese traveller Hieun Tsang described Kancheepuram as a place 'whose soil is fertile and regularly cultivated and produces an abundance of grain, where the climate is hot and the character of the people courageous'. What Hieun Tsang said so long ago still applies today.

Kancheepuram is the ancient Pallava capital and, because of the extant buildings of that period, is a treasure ground of Tamil temple architecture. Throughout the centuries it has been known for its silk-weaving industry, records of which go back to the fourteenth century. At

72 Arjuna's Penance, the world's largest bas-relief; at Mahabalipuram, Tamil Nadu

present, according to the 1983 count, there are as many as 12,000 silk looms in the district.

Kancheepuram is 75 km (47 miles) south-west of Madras and is the administrative centre of the Chingleput district; it is included in the itinerary of most of the tours of the area based on Madras.

Chidambaram
Here are set some of the oldest temples in India. Spread over 16 hectares (40 acres) is the great temple to Nataraj, dedicated to Lord Shiva in his cosmic dance form, Nataraj. It is not a place at which to stay over-night although there is a tourist bungalow; better to stay at nearby Kumbakonam

Kumbakonam
This is another city of great antiquity, famous for its gold work and its silver jewellery, for brass-ware and betel leaf. It is a pilgrim centre and seems always to be full of itinerant Indians, Swamis and mendicants. If you stand awhile by the bridge over the canal you can watch as naked local youths dive and leap from the bridge parapets into the rather noxious water below.

Gangaikondacholapuram
A great temple complex nearby Kumbakonum, it was built by the Emperor Rajendra Chola in the eleventh century AD in an effort to outdo his father, Raja Raja Chola's perfect creation, the Brehadeswara Temple at Tanjore. Here, nowadays, religion is all and this strange temple city is one of the places in the world where one can really escape all signs of modern life.

73 Brehadeswara Temple, Tanjore

Tanjore

Tanjore is the capital of the district of that name. Its 'modern' name is Tanjavur and its jewel is the glorious Chola temple called Brehadeswara. This temple really needs a whole day for visiting as there is so much to see. The *vimana*, or central tower, which soars above the *sanctum sanctorium* is 66 m (216 ft) high and is capped by a single block of granite which weighs 80 tons. It was placed into position by pulling it up a man-built incline that started 6 km (4 miles) away. There are beautiful murals, lingam shrines and a museum set in grounds reminiscent of a Daniels engraving. Soft browns and fawns mingle with pale green palms, frangipani and neem trees, the weathered stone and granite and exposed ferruginous bricks that shaped the whole before being either stone-clad or pargetted.

Tanjore is a musical city where instruments are made as well as being played and one can wander around the music bazaars and watch as craftsmen fashion sitars, tambouras and drums.

Madurai

A short bus journey from Tanjore, Madurai is known as the 'City of Nectar', *mathuram* being Tamil for nectar. The main attraction at Madurai is undoubtedly the great Meenakshi Temple. Unlike the simple beauty of plain stone, the whole of the Meenakshi Temple is painted in bright primary colours – as was customary on most southern temples when they were first created. It is the vast wealth of the Meenakshi Temple that allows this original tradition to be so well maintained.

Tirunelveli

Here is a massive temple, the Nellatappar Temple. It is not noteworthy, but the town is a good starting place from which to venture to more remote places in Tamil Nadu, such as Tuticorin on the coast, where the famous pearl fishers are. Tuticorin is now a modern port but down the coast are some fine safe sands for swimming and camping. At Cortallam, set among glorious forests at about 305 m (1000 ft), there are seven (the magic number) waterfalls that are believed to have curative properties. The main waterfall drops 91 m (300 ft) in three stages and provides some delightful cool showers for the hot walker. Go in late October through to January; later on the waters will have dried to a trickle.

Rameswaram

The great temple here has incredible corridors that enclose the sanctum, extending 1219 m (4000 ft). They are the longest in India. The Rama-nathaswamy Temple exhibits all the beauty, grace and intricacy of the

74 Meenakshi Temple, Madurai

75 Detail of ornate plaster work on temples at Madurai

Dravidian style in a perfect way, it is so well preserved. It is from Rameswaram that the ferry departs for Sri Lanka.

Kanya Kumari
The Land's End of India, this is a pilgrimage place for those who follow the teaching of Vivekananda. There is a memorial to him set out on a rock that looks strangely like St Paul's Cathedral. There are many-coloured sands to be found on the beaches here, and good swimming and hotels. Kanya Kumari can easily be visited from Kerala, from Trivandrum.

Tiruchirappalli
Better known, before Independence, as Trichinopoly or just Trichy, the unmistakable landmark is the Rock Temple which rises right in the middle of the town. It is a good climb to the top. The River Cauvery runs through Trichy separating it from Srirangam, a nearby temple city set amongst jungly trees. Seen from the top of the Rock Temple, its huge towering gopurams jut upwards through the foliage like the sails of galleons.

Trichy has several churches and many temples but it is its fascinating bazaars that make it alive and colourful. There is one street entirely devoted to the making and selling of artificial diamonds.

Whatever you do when here, do not fail to visit Srirangam, the temple

76 Part of the 1219 m (4000 ft) of corridors at the Ramanathaswamy Temple, Rameswaram

city only 5 km (3 miles) away (on a number 1 bus). At Srirangam is the thousand pillared hall and the Ranganatha temple with its façade row of monolithic columns carved out of single blocks of rose pink granite depicting rearing horses with warrior riders and their retinue. The detail today is as sharp as when it was carved, 400 years ago.

Coonoor
A half-way stop en route to Ooty, Coonoor can be reached either by local bus or, more interestingly, by the toy railway, the Blue Mountain Railway, which runs from Coimbatore. Be sure that the train is running, as sometimes there is a shortage of coal!

Ootacamund
Described in the brochure as 'a fairy-land of cloud-kissed peaks, dense forests, rushing streams and undulating emerald-green downs', Ooty

77 Part of the Srirangam Temple near Trichinopoly

pleases everyone who goes there. Dodabetta Peak crowns Ooty (2712 m [8900 ft]) with magnificent views and wild rhododendron, the vistas having a blue sheen, hence the name Nilgiri, meaning blue mountains. (For a more detailed description, see the earlier section on hill stations on pp. 54–8.

Pondicherry

Pondicherry is 257 km (159 miles) south of Madras on the east coast of India. A one-time village called Puddicherri, it used to trade with the Romans and, by this trading and meeting of peoples, became a place of

78 The Rock Fort Temple at Trichinopoly

learning. European traders were attracted to what became known as Pondycherry, a corruption of the old Tamil name, because it offered alternative safe anchorage to Madras, and soon it became a well-known port of call on the Coromandel coast.

In 1673 François Martin, a French trader who had a great deal of experience of India, bought the still relatively small trading community, then called Pudducherri, from its owner, the Rajah of Bijapur, and its expansion as a port began. The French company was formed and enjoyed peaceful trading, although not without the need to defend its position. There were many skirmishes with marauding ships off the coast. Pondicherry represented a valuable prize to both Dutch and British traders. It finally ceded defeat to the British after the battle of Wandewash. The French withstood an eight month siege, after which, on 16 January, 1761, Governor Lally capitulated to the British commander, Sir Eyre Coote.

This date effectively ended French power in India. By 1783 Pondicherry and the enclave was declared an open town, similar in position to Trieste. The enclave went from French to British to French control until it was restored to the French in title, under the 1802 Treaty of Amiens. The French allowed the British, who had founded trading interests, to stay on, and harmony prevailed. Pondicherry became a free enclave within India, under the British. In 1817 the British gave it back to the French Government and the territory that was once walked by the Romans, and was to be subsequently the subject of so many machinations, settled down to a long and peaceful trading era.

During the Second World War the people of Pondicherry declared their support for de Gaulle, and the area was then used as a base for allied operations against Japan. After Indian Independence in 1947, the French stayed autonomous until 1954, when they handed over the administration to the Indian Government. Pondicherry and the other French possessions of Karikal, Yanaon and Mahé were finally handed over to India in 1962. This amounted to a total of 470 sq. km (181 sq. miles). Today, Pondicherry has a population of 600,000; when restored to the French Government in 1817 it had only 25,000. The French left in 1962 and offered alternative citizenship to the Franco-Indian peoples of the enclaves; 50 per cent opted to keep French nationality – one half of the total of the native and European population.

The town is laid out on the grid system, separated into halves by a sludgy canal that runs parallel with the sea about 1200 m (3937 ft) inland. There is the sea side and the inland side. The French named the former *ville blanche* and the latter *ville noire*. The ville blanche is a mixture of leftover French respectability inoculated with a liberal colouring of Indian opportunism. In fact, the native town is native whereas the old French town is a mixture. That this mixture has not been more dominated by the native Tamilians is due to the enormous influence of the Aurobindo Ashram.

Nowadays, the Ashram and its activities is the raison d'être for most of the visitors to Pondicherry. It is off the beaten track and off the tourist track. You have to travel to Madras, in the south, and then entrain from Egmore Station. The train, which is now a through service, stops en route at various small places, and arrives at Pondicherry four hours later.

The Ashram sprang from an unusual beginning and has a world-wide following. Its founder, Sri Aurobindo, was born in Calcutta in 1872, on 15 August. When he was seven years old he was taken to England to be educated and in 1890 went up to King's College, Cambridge. In 1893 he was back in India and became involved in the more extreme wing of the Indian Independence Movement. As a writer and revolutionary, he organized the publication of his journal, *Bande Mataram*, and through it became a powerful anti-British voice: anti the British Government, not the British.

He was jailed by the British in 1908 for his involvement in a bomb plot. While in prison, he meditated and studied yoga. Perhaps disillusioned with the political struggle and feeling let down by others, he was struck by an intense spiritual awakening on his release from prison in 1910, and retired from politics to quiet and solitude in Pondicherry, away from British jurisdiction, rejecting political overtures from active Independence parties.

By 1920 he had formed his teaching philosophies, started the Ashram, and had been joined by 'the Mother'. She was a French woman called Mira Alfassa who had visited Pondicherry in 1914 and had met Aurobindo, who created a lasting impression upon her. After travelling round the world, she left her home in Paris, went to Pondicherry, and never returned to France. She associated herself totally with the work of the Ashram and eventually, in 1926, commenced the running of it herself. Sri Aurobindo had retired into seclusion to pursue his personal meditations and to evolve his writings. He died in 1950; the Mother lived on until 1973.

The principles that guide the Ashram are integrated living and working together, seeking a higher consciousness.

The Ashram has bought more than 400 houses in Pondicherry; it is said that the Ashram *is* Pondicherry. Two thousand people make up the Ashram community and live and work there in the many buildings which are spread around the town and countryside. There is a brick factory, mosaic works, a printing press and a paper-making factory. Pottery, cottage industries, hand-weaving, stainless steel making, bee keeping, an oil mill, a dispensary, two hospitals, a theatre and gymnasium and many other activities keep the 2000 people working in order to support the Ashram and its main work, education. The Sri Aurobindo Centre of Education is the most important part of the Ashram.

Aurobindo's belief was that man is not yet in his final stage of development, and that the ascending evolution of nature – stone to plant to animals and to man – has another stage to go. He claimed that man in his present form is so imperfect that nature could not be satisfied with the result and will endeavour to evolve a being who will be to man what man is to the animal world.

An Ashram originally meant a place where a master lived and his disciples came to listen. To quote from a handout: 'the spirit behind the Ashram was not one of barren self-denial, but rather one of glad acceptance of life and all its possibilities'. The same handout says, later on: 'The Sri Aurobindo Ashram has the same catholic and dynamic character', meaning the same universal desire to seek a greater awareness of supramentality.

It is interesting that later in her life the Mother outlawed sex. There seemed no reason why she imposed celibacy upon the community, and it was an odd thing for her to do as she was so worldly. Perhaps she saw too many of the wrong people joining the way of life in Pondicherry and wished to discourage them by imposing the extra discipline as a necessity for achieving ultimate enlightenment. Like every restriction, however, the ban on sex is ignored by many.

There are other aspects of Pondicherry. The Romain Rolland Library in the rue Capucine contains a large collection of rare books and manuscripts. Founded in 1827, it has, conveniently next door, the Archaeological Museum containing artefacts from Poduca and Arikamedu, important Roman trading posts. There is the European cemetery with a fair number of tombs of 'enfants morts' and ornate marble excesses associated with nineteenth-century French Catholic grief. The Botanical Gardens were laid down in 1826 and are now resplendent with unusual indigenous trees as well as specimens imported from all over the world.

There are few cars, the main form of transport being the bicycle. Public carriers are invariably cycle-rickshaws. Joan of Arc waves a flag outside the Eglise de Notre Dame des Anges in the rue Dumas. Along the promenade is the Gandhi memorial; he stands under a sort of temple d'amour, surrounded by enormous carved pillars which come from Gingee Fort, away in the hills to the west. A new, modern pier, ugly as such things almost always are, juts into the sea at the end of the broad promenade which is lined by gardens and graceful villas.

A few miles south of Pondicherry lies Arikamedu, an archaeological site excavated in parts by Sir Mortimer Wheeler. It is Indo-Roman, dating back to the second century BC. After Sir Mortimer Wheeler's team departed, the site was neglected. In 1982 the Government declared the site a protected area. It is in a beautiful setting amidst casuarina trees on the bank of the river called Arikamhuppam. Ostensibly it is the oldest archaeological site in south India.

Pondicherry, by its isolation, spirituality, purpose and history, is a unique experience. Contrary to its sleepy prospect, it is a hive of industry and does not encourage idleness. It is not a place to which to escape.

This Coromandel coast has a double monsoon, one from the east during July, August and September, and a western rainfall in December. It is always warm, and in summer it can be scorching.

Glossary

When compiling a glossary of words particular to India, not only is there a multiplicity of languages within the sub-continent to consider, but there is also the wide use of English.

The word for 'sugar' will be 'sugar' in one area, 'chini' in another and 'sacar' in yet another. The word for horse-drawn cart or passenger vehicle may be 'tonga', 'ekka' or 'jakta', depending on the location in India. In this glossary, though, only one version is given.

It may surprise some readers to find how many words are used in the English language that have their origins in either Sanskrit or Urdu. Here is a contrived piece to illustrate this, the 'foreign' words being in italics:

A *Swami* sat on the *verandah* of the *bungalow*; by him was a *teak* table on which was some *rice* and *curry* and a plate of *kedgeree*, plus a jar of *chutney*. A *Guru* called and sat on *chintz* cushions, and a pupil joined them wearing *khaki dungarees, sandals* and *shawl*. A servant in *mufti* served fruit *punch*. After his guests left, the *Swami shampooed* his hair, did some *yoga* exercises and then, clad in *pyjamas*, went to bed.

Religious

Acharaya	Teacher, or spiritual guide
Ahisma	Non-violence
Ashram	Saintly place of learning
Avatar	Name given to various incarnations of Vishnu
Bhagavad Gita	Part of the Mahabharata (q.v.)
Brahma	Hindu creator of all things
Brahmin	Priestly and first caste in Hinduism
Caste	Hindu hereditary class system
Dharamsala	Religious rest house, without amenities
Dharma	The path of earthly conduct
Fakir	Muslim or Hindu religious mendicant
Granth Sahib	Sacred book of Sikhs
Guru	Spiritual teacher
Haji	Muslim who has made the pilgrimage to Mecca
Harijan	Below caste; previously called Untouchable
Hatha Yoga	Physical exercise plus spiritual discipline
Imam	Muslim religious leader
Juggernauts	Huge decorated temple carts
Kshatriya	Warrior caste; second caste in Hinduism
Lama	Tibetan Buddhist priest
Lingam	Phallic symbol; sacred symbol of Shiva
Mahabharata	Vedic scriptures – the principal Hindu holy book
Mantra	Word or sentence used as invocation
Muezzin	One who calls Muslims to prayer

Mullah	Muslim priest
Nirvana	State of total peace
Pooja	Prayer before the Gods
Pranayama	Study of breathing control
Prasad	Food of the Gods
Qur'an	Koran, the scripture of Mohammed, Muslim holy book
Rath	Temple chariot
Rishi	Holy man
Sadhu	Celibate holy man
Samadhi	Memorial of cremation
Shakti	Life force through spirituality
Sudra	Fourth and lowest caste in Hinduism
Swami	Teacher within Hinduism
Tirthankars	The 24 Jain patriarchs
Upanishads	Ancient Vedic scriptures
Vedas	Four most ancient Hindu writings
Yoga	Discipline of exercise and meditation
Yoni	Female fertility symbol

Architectural

Anikut	A dam
Bagh	A garden
Baoli	Deep well with steps and galleries
Bund	Embankment of river
Bundar	Port or harbour
Cantonment	Military and administrative area in the time of the British
Chaitya	Buddhist temple or prayer hall
Chatri	Tomb or mausoleum
Cutchery	Building for public business
Darwaza	Gateway to a city, or simply a door
Diwan-i-Am	Hall of public audience
Diwan-i-Khas	Hall of private audience
Dravidian	South Indian architectural style
Ghat	Steps leading to water
Godown	Locked store room
Gopuram	Monumental pyramidical gateway leading into south Indian temples
Haveli	Large houses with interior courtyards
Howdah	Seat on back of elephant for carrying people
Kothi	Name for private house or mansion
Mahal	Palace
Maidan	Open space, generally grassed
Mandapam	Porch of a Hindu temple
Mandir	Hindu temple

Masjid	Muslim mosque
Math	Monastery
Mithuna	Statues of amorous couples
Nagar	Town
Nandi	Bull; vehicle of Shiva; found in temples such as at Mysore and Tanjore
Ojila	Muslim fort
Punkah	Ceiling fan pulled by rope
Rickshaw	Vehicle drawn by either man, cycle or motor
Serai	Cheap accommodation for travellers
Stupa	Buddhist sacred mound
Tank	Water storage lake
Vihar	Place of learning
Vimana	Main centre of Hindu temple; *sanctum sanctorium*
Zenana	Secluded place for women in Muslim house

Food and drink

Alu	Potato
Anda	Egg
Arrack	Alcoholic drink made from coconut milk or rice
Atta	Wholemeal flour
Bombay duck	Small gelatinous fish found in Bay of Bengal and Bombay areas; dried in sun and served crisp or salted or pickled
Biriyani	Layers of partly-boiled rice between which are put meat or vegetables before being baked
Chai	Tea to drink
Chapati	Bread made of unfermented wheat dough
Chat	Name for snacks
Chini	Sugar
Dansak	Parsee preparation of rice and curry
Dhal	Lentils cooked in a variety of ways
Dood	Milk
Doodpak	Pudding made of rice, sugar, milk and cardamon
Dopiaza	Meat in thick sauce twice boiled with lots of onions
Dosa	Savoury pancake made with fermented batter of ground lentils and rice
Fenni	Alcoholic drink made from the cashew 'apple'
Firnee	Creamy pudding made of rice flour, milk and almonds or pistachio nuts
Ghee	Clarified butter
Gulab jamun	Sweet balls of curd in rose syrup
Halwa	Sweetmeat made of lentil, semolina, carrot or pumpkin, with milk and sugar
Idli	Fermented mixture of lentil and rice steamed in moulds

Inam	Rice
Jaggery	Boiled-down juice of sugar-cane, like soft brown sugar
Jalebi	Convoluted deep-fried pancake mixture steeped in boiling sugar-water
Kafi	Coffee
Keema	Minced meat
Kheer	Sweet milk pudding
Kofta	Minced meat or vegetable balls in sauce
Korma	Thick curry enriched with ground poppy seeds and desiccated coconut
Lassi	Drink made from yoghurt and water plus flavour
Machli	Fish
Makkhan	Butter
Masala	Indian condiments and spices
Mithai	Sweet
Murghi	Chicken
Muttar	Peas
Nan	Indian bread
Pan	Mixture of lime, betel nut and spices and sometimes tobacco folded in a betel leaf secured with a clove; eaten as a digestive
Pani	Water
Paneer	Cheese
Parotha	Fried bread made from wheat flour
Payasam	Milk pudding made from vermicelli
Pomfret	Bombay fish, similar to sole
Pulao	Rice fried in ghee and then cooked in stock
Raita	Raw vegetables chopped and mixed with yoghurt
Rasam	Spicy soup
Ras gulla	Sweet white milky balls in cardamon sauce
Rogan josh	Curried mutton or lamb
Sambar	Lentil and vegetable preparation, sharp and spicy
Samosa	Envelopes of curried meat and/or vegetables which are deep-fried
Shah jahani	Dish garnished with beaten silver leaf
Srikand	Dehydrated curd mixed with sugar and flavoured with cardamons
Subji	Vegetables
Tandoor	Deep oven
Tandoori	Barbecued spiced meat cooked in a tandoor
Toddy	Alcoholic drink made from palm flower 'milk'

General

Ayah	Children's nurse
Baksheesh	A tip or bribe

Banian	Vest
Bearer	Personal servant
Begum	Muslim lady of high rank
Betel	Nut of the betel palm (areca)
Bhisti	Water carrier
Burka	Black garment covering orthodox Muslim women
Chappals	Sandals
Chela	Pupil
Chelo	Come on! Go on! Get going!
Charpoi	Indian rope bed
Choli	Blouse worn as undergarment by women
Chowk	Market place
Crore	Of rupees – equals ten million
Dawa	Medicine
Dhoti	Skirt-like cloth tied round waist and pulled up between the legs
Dooli	Litter for carrying infirm or elderly; carried by four men holding poles; like palanquin
Durbar	A royal court
Gaddi	Throne of royalty
Ghari	Carriage, or motorized vehicle
Ghazal	Urdu love song
Gopi	Milk-maid, prosaically a cowherd girl
Hartal	Strike of labour force
Hookah	Hubble-bubble water pipe for smoking tobacco
Ji	Honorific suffix to name, hence 'Gandhiji'
Ji	Yes
Kadi	Homespun cloth
Kameeze	Trouser-like garment worn by Muslim women
Kripiya	Please
Lakh	Of rupees – equals one hundred thousand
Lathi	Indian policeman's control stick
Lingam	Phallic symbol of Lord Shiva
Lok	The people
Lunghi	Cloth wrapped around the loins
Mahout	Elephant master
Mali	Gardener
Mantra	Prayer
Mela	Fair
Munshi	Secretary
Namaste	Indian greeting: Good morning, afternoon, evening or Good day
Nahi	No
Nawab	Governor
Pandit	Wise man or master of particular subject
Peon	Lower grade clerical worker

Phul	Flower
Raga	Theme for musical variations
Rajput	Hindu warrior of Rajasthan
Sahib	Title applied to any man in authority
Salwar	Blouse worn by Muslim women
Sepoy	Private in the infantry
Shikar	Hunting
Shikara	Small boat paddled on Lake Dal, Kashmir
Shukriya	Thank you
Suttee	The act of self-immolation by a widow on her husband's funeral pyre. Though now outlawed, the practice is still carried on.
Syce	Groom of horses
Tonga	Horse-drawn cart
Wallah	A person, suffixed to trades; for instance, 'officewallah'
Zamindar	Rich landowner

Bibliography

ARCHER, M., *Indian Architecture and the British*, Thames and Hudson, 1976

BOURKE-WHITE, M., *Interview with India*, Phoenix House, 1950

CARROLL, D., *The Taj Mahal*, Reader's Digest, 1972

COLLINS, J. & LAPIERE, D., *Freedom at Midnight*, Collins, 1975

CRAVEN, R. C., *Concise History of Indian Art*, Thames & Hudson, 1976

DOWSON, J., *Classical Dictionary of Hindu Mythology*, Routledge & Kegan Paul, 1968

DROUBIE, R. EL, *Islam*, Ward Lock Educational, 1970

EDWARDS, M., *Indian Temples and Palaces*, Hamlyn, 1969

FISHLOCK, T., *India File*, Murray, 1983

GASCOIGNE, B., *The Great Moghuls*, Cape, 1971

GRANT, W. J., *Spirit of India*, Batsford, 1938

HAMBLEY, G., *Cities of Mughal India*, Elek, 1968

HUTTON, J. H., *Caste in India*, Cambridge University Press, 1946

IONS, V., *Myths and Legends of India*, Hamlyn, 1970

KEAY, J., *India Discovered*, Windward, 1983

KEAY, J., *Into India*, Murray, 1973

LEWIS, B., *The World of Islam*, Thames & Hudson, 1976

LORD, J., *The Maharajahs*, Hutchinson, 1972

MEHTA, V., *Portrait of India*, Penguin, 1950

MOORHOUSE, G., *India Britannica*, Harvil Press, 1982

MURPHY, D., *On a Shoestring to Coorg*, Murray, 1976

NAIPAUL, V. S. *An Area of Darkness*, Deutsch, 1964

NATH, A., *Goa*, Vikas (New Delhi), 1970

PANDEY, B. N., *A Book of India*, Collins, 1981

PANTER-DOWNES, M., *Ooty Preserved*, Hamilton, 1967
RAWSON, P., *Indian Asia*, Elsevier-Phaidon, 1977
RUSHBROOK WILLIAMS, L. F., *A Handbook for Travellers in India, Pakistan, Burma and Ceylon*, Murray, 1958
SASTRI, K. A. N., *A History of South India*, Oxford University Press, 1955
SEN, K. M., *Hinduism*, Pelican, 1961
SINGH, R., *Kashmir – Garden of the Himalayas*, Perenial Press, 1983
SMITH, V. A., *The Oxford History of India*, 3rd edition, Oxford University Press, 1958
SPEAR, SIR P., *A History of India, Vol. II*, Pelican, 1966 (for Vol. I, see THAPAR)
SPEAR, SIR P., *Twilight of the Mughuls*, Cambridge University Press, 1951
THAPAR, R., *A History of India, Vol. I*, Pelican, 1966 (for Vol. II, see SPEAR)
WATSON, F., *A Concise History of India*, Thames & Hudson, 1974
WILES, J., *Delhi is Far Away*, Elek, 1974
WOODCOCK, G., *Faces of India*, Faber, 1964
WOODCOCK, G., *Kerala*, Faber, 1967
YOUNGHUSBAND, F., *Kashmir*, A. & C. Black, 1917

Index

Agra   105–6
  Jami Masjid   105
  Red Fort   105–6, 123
  Taj Mahal   48, 81, 105–6, 108, 148
Ahmedabad   133–5
  Jami Masjid   133
Ajmer   127
Akbar   107–8, 149
Allahabad   108–9
Almora   105
Alwar   133
Amber   125, 127
  Amber Palace   125–7
Amritsar   98
  Golden Temple   42, 98
  Jallianwala Bogh   98
Andra Pradesh   19, 24, 150, 163–7
Asoka, Emperor   39, 117, 118, 146
Assam   19, 23, 112, 122
astrology   30–1
Aurobindo Ashram   181–3

Bangalore   153
Baroda   135–6
Bay of Bengal   14, 119
Belur   156
Bengal (*see* West Bengal)
Benares (Varanasi)   109–11
Bharatpur   133
Bhopal   144
Bhubaneswar   19, 119
  Great Lingaraj Temple   119, 120
Bihar   15, 19, 21, 22, 64, 112, 117

Bijapur   155
  Gol Gumbaz   155
Bikaner   131
birds   83–5, 137 (*see also* game sanctuaries)
Bombay   14, 19, 24, 43, 46, 139–41
  Elephanta Island   139
  Towers of Silence   140
Bramhaputra   23
Buddhism   37–40, 58, 118, 143
  Lord Buddha   21, 24, 35, 37–8, 61, 111, 146
  temples   132
Bundi   132

Calcutta   14, 52, 112–15
  Black Hole   115
caste   34, 41
Central Government   27–9 (*see also* politics)
Chali   99
Chandigarh   19, 98
Charnock, Job   113
Chidambaram   175
Chilka Lake   120
Chittorgarh   129
  Tower of Victory   129, 130
Chorwad   137–8
Christianity   20, 24, 30, 36
cinema   30, 89–92
climate   9, 13, 16–17, 21, 24, 48, 56–7, 104, 120, 123, 141, 147, 153
climbing plants   81–3
Cochin   170-2
  Jewish Synagogue   170
Congress Party   20, 28 (*see also* politics)

Curzon, Lord 119

dacoity 24
dancing 87-9, 163
Darjeeling 14, 23, 50, 58, 112, 115-17
Dehra Dun 105
Delhi (*see* New Delhi, Old Delhi)
Dhar 149
Dharamsala 99
Dravidians 15, 16, 17, 23, 152
Dwarka 137

Emergency, the 28
emigration 17, 168

farming 15, 21, 30, 99-100, 116, 122, 133, 150,
    163, 168
Fatehpur Sikri 107-8
    Buland Darwaza 107
    Hiram Minar 107
food and drink 69, 70-3, 152

game sanctuaries 56, 65-7, 172
Gangaikondacholapuram 175
Ganges 14, 15, 21, 64, 101, 104, 108, 109-10,
    117, 118
    Gangetic Plain 13, 21
Ghandi
    Indira 28, 44
    Mahatma 133, 134, 137, 141
    Rajiv 19, 28
    Sanjay 28
Goa 19, 48, 150-2
Golconda 164
Gujarat 13, 14, 19, 23, 24, 43, 45, 65, 122,
    133-8
Gwalior 144-5

Halebid 156
Harappan civilization 14, 17
Hardwar 102, 104
Harijans 30, 34
Haryana 19, 20, 93, 98-9
hill stations 21, 49, 54-8, 73, 98, 105, 131, 142,
    147, 166, 172, 179-80
Himachal Pradesh 19, 93, 99-101
Himalayas 13, 14, 73, 99, 100, 115
Hinduism 27, 29, 30, 33-5, 40, 58-9, 60, 62, 89,
    98, 109, 119, 137, 159, 162, 166, 172
    Hindus 15, 20, 41, 65, 71, 108, 109, 131, 137,
        144, 147, 158, 159, 160, 162
    monuments 142, 144, 151, 155, 175
Hyderabad 163-5
    Char Minar 163-4

Independence 10, 14, 17, 21, 34, 41, 49, 61, 95,
    102, 119, 140, 144, 154, 178, 181
Indore 147
industry 21, 24, 139-40, 143, 163, 164
infant mortality 17
Islam 35-7, 58, 63, 106, 154, 155, 163
    Muslims 30, 41, 71, 73, 80, 108, 144, 149,
        158, 159, 160, 161
    shrines 151

Jagannath, Lord 119-20
Jai Singh 133
Jainism 40, 58
    temples 131-2, 134, 137, 138, 142, 146
    Jains 40, 133, 147, 155
Jaipur 123-5
    City Palace 124-5
    Janta Mantar 125
Jaisalmer 131
Jammu and Kashmir 19, 93-7 (*see also*
    Kashmir)
Jamnagar 136
Jhansi 145-6
Jodhpur 129
judicial system 27-8
Jumna 108
Junagadh 136

Kalahasti 166
Kalimpong 117
Kancheepuram 174-5
Kanya Kumari 13, 178
Karnataka 19, 24, 150, 152-63
Kashmir 13, 20, 21, 93-7
Kerala 19, 24, 27, 29, 32, 166, 168-72
Khajuraho 146-7
Kodaikanal 56-7
Konarak 119
Kotah 132
Kovalum 168-9
Krishnamurthy, J. 173
Kulu 99-101
Kumbakonam 175
Kutch 137

Lake Jaisamund 129
languages 18
Le Corbusier 98
literacy 29, 168
Lonavala 141
Lucknow 108
Lutyens, Sir Edward 102

Madhya Pradesh 19, 23, 24, 138
Madras 172, 174
Madurai 177
    Meenakshi Temple 177
Mahabaleshwar 57-8, 142
Maharastra 19, 138-43
Manali 101
Mandu 147-50
    Jahaz Mahal 148-9
    Mandu Plateau 150
Mangalagiri 166, 167
    Lakshminarasinah Swami 167
Manipur 19
Meghalaya 19
minerals 15, 112, 143
Moghul Empire 108, 127, 144, 149
Mohenjo-Daro 14
monsoon 29, 148, 183
morality 30
Mount Abu 57, 131
music 86-7, 163, 177

Muslims (*see* Islam)
Mussorie 55, 105
Mysore 34, 154

Nagaland 19
Naina Tal 105
Nehru, Jawaharlal 19, 20
Nepal 21, 23
New Delhi 15, 20, 101–3
  Red Fort 102, 103
North Eastern Indian Territories 112, 122

Old Delhi 102–3
  Jami Jasjid 102
  Jantar Mantar 102–3
Ootacamund 56, 179–80
opium 118
Orchcha 145–6
Orissa 19, 112, 118–20

Pachmari 147
Pakistan 13, 14, 21, 41, 49, 95, 106, 122
panchayat 27, 31–2
Parsees 42–4, 59, 71, 139, 140
Partition, the 14
Patna 117, 118
  Bodh Gaya 21, 39, 118
photography 73–5, 131
pilgrimages 65, 101, 109, 118, 131, 137, 156, 166, 175, 178
Politana 137, 138
politics 27–9
  Communist Party 29
  Congress Party 20, 28
  Janata Party 28–9
  Separatism 20
Pondicherry 19, 180–3
Poona 141
population 16–17 (*see also* emigration)
Porbander 137
Punjab 19, 20, 21, 41, 93, 97–8, 101
Puri 119–20
Pushkar 131

Rajasthan 18, 19, 21, 22, 50, 64, 73, 122–3
Rajkot 137
Rameswaram 177–8
  Ramanathaswamy Temple 177–8, 179
religion 33–44 (*see also under individual names*)
Rishikesh 104–5

Sanchi 146
Sawai Jai Singh 123–5
Seringapatnam 155–6
sexuality 30, 117
Shah Jehan 102, 105–6, 108, 127, 148

shikara 94, 95
Shiva, Lord 33, 110, 129, 147, 175
shrubs 79–80
Sikhism 40, 41–2, 58
  Sikhs 21, 71, 97
Sikkim 19, 122
Siliguri 117
silk 153, 172, 175
Simla 21, 55–6, 99
smuggling 21, 23, 117
Sravanabelgola 156, 157
States, the 18–27
Suez Canal 49
suttee 110, 129

Taj Mahal 48, 81, 105–6, 148
Tamil Nadu 19, 24, 26, 45, 166, 172–83
Tanjore 176–7
  Brehadeswara Temple 176–7
television 92
Tipu Sultan 155, 156, 157
Tiruchirappally (Trichinopoly) 178–9
  Rock Fort 170, 180
  Srirangam Temple 179–80
Tirunelveli 177
Tirupathi 164, 166
Tiruttani 166
trading 14–15, 158, 162, 178, 180–1, 182
travel 45–54
  by air 48, 52–3, 115, 150
  by bus and coach 48, 53–4, 131, 158, 174
  by rail 48–52, 56, 57, 58, 99, 116, 117, 131, 141, 150, 179
  health 46, 67–73
  routes to India 46–7
trees 76–9, 148, 154
Tripura 19
Trivandrum 168, 169

Udaipur 128
  Palace 128
Ujain 147
Undying Banyan Tree 109
Uttar Pradesh 19, 21, 101–11

Varanasi (*see* Benares)
video 48, 54, 92, 174
Vijayanagar 158–63
  Pampapati Temple 158, 159
village life 20, 29–32
Vindhya Mountains 143, 147, 148
Vizagapatnam 166

Waltair 166
West Bengal 13, 19, 29, 112–17.

1/N